Ghassoub Sharif Mustafa holds an Ed.D. (Doctor of Education), an MA, a BA, and a Certificate in Management, and has attained the rank of an Associate Professor of English and he speaks three languages. The author has taught English and liberal arts for more than four decades to Arab and international higher education students. Ghassoub is interested in reviving the habit of reading in the Arab World, and in promoting a global community that shares the same basic human values and principles.

For my wife, Sanaa, my children, Amaal, Ramzy, Nabil, my granddaughter, Haya, and all Sharif's children and grandchildren in Palestine and all over the world.

I dedicate this book to those individuals who helped me enter the English language world to rise from a miserable ABC learner to become a professor of English and an author. Charlotte, the English lady at the Dead sea, who taught me my first English words and phrases, and predicted that I would be a gentle Englishman one day. My first English teacher, Mr. Waleed, who taught me English in grade 5. He was the first teacher ever to make a school subject relevant to our life. The big-hearted official at the embassy, who made me stick to the English department and made me turn failure into success. My professors at the Faculté des langues étrangères, faculty of foreign languages, Oran University, who were patient, tolerant, and extremely supportive.

I also dedicate this book to my adoptive mother, the English language because she inspired me and empowered me to write this book. Although she was harsh and uncompromising while educating me and teaching me her strict rules and unique style in the beginning, I did not hate her nor had a grudge against her because I knew her good intentions. English, my adoptive mother, made me from nothing to something. She guided me and held a torch for me during my darkest nights when I was trying to sail in her vast roaring seas. She stood with me against oppression. She told some of her arrogant native speakers that she was not the property of anyone and warned them to stop harassing me and keep their hands off me. She declared that she was the mother of all oppressed people in the world. And when the right time came, she opened her treasure for me and asked me to help myself.

Ghassoub Sharif Mustafa

MY ENGLISH LANGUAGE JOURNEY

From Beginner to Professor and Author

AUSTIN MACAULEY PUBLISHERS™

LONDON * CAMBRIDGE * NEW YORK * SHARJAH

Copyright © Ghassoub Sharif Mustafa 2023

The right of Ghassoub Sharif Mustafa to be identified as author of this work has been asserted by the author in accordance with Federal Law No. (7) of UAE, Year 2002, Concerning Copyrights and Neighbouring Rights.

All rights reserved. No part of this publication may be reproduced, stored in a retrieval system, or transmitted in any form or by any means, electronic, mechanical, photocopying, recording, or otherwise, without the prior permission of the publishers.

Any person who commits any unauthorised act in relation to this publication may be liable to legal prosecution and civil claims for damages.

All of the events in this memoir are true to the best of author's memory. The views expressed in this memoir are solely those of the author.

The age group that matches the content of the books has been classified according to the age classification system issued by the Ministry of Culture and Youth.

ISBN – 9789948778189 – (Paperback)
ISBN – 9789948778196 – (E-Book)

Application Number: MC-10-01-9621037
Age Classification: E

Printer Name: iPrint Global Ltd
Printer Address: Witchford, England

First Published 2023
AUSTIN MACAULEY PUBLISHERS FZE
Sharjah Publishing City
P.O Box [519201]
Sharjah, UAE
www.austinmacauley.ae
+971 655 95 202

My sincerest thanks to Dr. Elizabeth Howell from New Zealand, friend, former colleague, Doctor of English and Education, and author, for editing the entire manuscript of this book, and for her input and constructive feedback. I am indebted to her genuine efforts and hard work.

Table of Contents

Prologue	12
Chapter 1: My Very First Word in English	17
Chapter 2: The English Woman in a Bikini at the Dead Sea	26
Chapter 3: Learning My ABC	35
Chapter 4: Oliver Twist of Jordan	42
Chapter 5: "Study English Because You Have the Right Aptitude"	49
Chapter 6: Be a Doctor or an Engineer or Disappear	60
Chapter 7: My Writing Struggle and the 'I' Grade	64
Chapter 8: The Wise Man Who Changed my Destiny	74
Chapter 9: Defeating the English Language	79
Chapter 10: From the American Dream to a Nation that Will Not Die	92
Chapter 11: The English Word is Mightier than the Sword	98
Chapter 12: The Cooperation Between My French and My English	102
Chapter 13: Learn English and Know Your Enemy	106
Chapter 14: From I Know My ABC To Teaching ABC	113
Chapter 15: Teaching Beyond *ABC and How Do You Do*	119
Chapter 16: Why Arab Learners Suffer More While Learning English	125
Chapter 17: The Hidden Battle for The English Classroom	133
Chapter 18: You Can Sell Ice to An Ice-Seller	140
Chapter 19: The Best Teacher Is a Storyteller	144

Chapter 20: The 7 Habits of Highly Effective Teachers   157

Chapter 21: My English – Arabic Poetry   167

Chapter 22: From a Miserable ABC Learner to an Author   179

Epilogue   189

Let's Recite Some Wisdom

"A journey of a thousand miles begins with a single step."
— **Confucius**

"Remember your dreams and fight for them. You must know what you want from life. There is just one thing that makes your dream impossible: the fear of failure."
— **Paulo Coelho, author of Al-Chemist, a best seller.**

"Learn a language, and you'll avoid a war."
— **Arab proverb**

"He who has mastered another nation's language, has acquired immunity against their evil."
— **Prophet Muhammad.** *Peace be upon him.*

"The difference between a successful person and others is not a lack of strength, not a lack of knowledge, but rather a lack in will."
— **Vince Lombardi Jr.**

"Success is no accident. It is hard work, perseverance, learning, studying, sacrificing and most of all, love of what you are doing or learning to do."
— **Pele**

"It does not matter how slowly you go as long as you do not stop."
— **Confucius**

"You don't always win, but every time you lose, you get better."
— **Ian Somerhalder**

"If you talk to a man in a language he understands, that goes to his head. If you talk to him in his own language, that goes to his heart."
— **Nelson Mandela.**

Prologue

While I was sipping my morning coffee with my wife one morning, she interrupted our daily conversation about news, children, picnics, my BBC, Gulf News, Al Bayan News, local and international news, and said, "Again, you were dreaming last night, and you were talking so loudly that I had difficulty sleeping."

As usual, I felt guilty about being naughty while sleeping and disturbing her. I apologised as that was out of my control. She giggled and tapped me on the shoulder and whispered in my ear, "It is under your control, dear."

"How?" I protested. "No one could control their dreams."

She commented calmly, "If you give your obsession with politics up, you will control your dreams."

"What has politics to do with dreams?" I wondered.

"Because most of your dreams are about politics." She giggled again. "So, if you forget politics, you may dream less, and I'll get more peaceful nights," she said.

I shook my head in agreement and felt crushed. "You are right," I confessed.

"You should thank your God that my dreams take place in the political arena rather than in the battlefield," I said.

My wife ululated and said loudly, "In the battlefield! I think I would rush out of bed in the middle of the night looking for protection."

We laughed out loud.

"But don't call the police."

I took another sip of my coffee and amusingly asked about the previous night dream and whether I was lecturing politics.

"Last night, you were not lecturing, you were hallucinating and talking to someone, but I repeatedly heard you were mentioning something like…Reagan…hay Reagan…"

"Oh! You mean Reagan, the American President," I said excitedly.

"I don't know. You were mentioning that name repeatedly."

I paused, looked at her, and said, "That is true; I was debating with him, if I remember, the hottest potato in the world: the historical rights of Palestinians and Israelis in Palestine."

"Did you convince him?"

"You're joking! How could I remember? Why don't you ask me if I had lunch at the White House? But I think it was a rough discussion."

"He was adamant that Palestinians had never existed and never stood out as nation," I said bitterly.

"You know, as usual I shouted, yelled and tried to argue. You know how agitated I become."

"Of course, I know how excited you get when you talk politics. You become like a toro in corrida and God help those that cross your path. Your horns are very sharp," she joked.

We both laughed heartily.

I laughed again. I like my wife's sense of humour.

"But my debate with Jimmy Carter was more peaceful because, in his book 'Palestine Not Apartheid,' he showed some sympathy toward Palestinians and called for justice."

"Oh! I did not hear that debate," my wife said.

"Perhaps you were asleep," I said giggling.

"He dared to criticise Israel because he had already left the White House," she said mockingly.

"Exactly."

I complained that people do not listen and that is why my debates turn into bullfights.

She suddenly said, "But you know what, last night you were talking in English in your dream. And no single word in Arabic. Of course, you were babbling sometimes and saying unintelligible things."

"I think I had been watching the news on the BBC before going to bed last night. I watched Reagan rallying for Israel and I hated him," I murmured.

"Ah! That's it. You watched the BBC, as usual, in English, of course. That is the BBC syndrome. They make you dream of their news because you love them."

"You know! I hate the BBC; I feel it's my rival, your second wife," she added.

"Polygamy is allowed in Islam," I said.

Do you know why I started my book by that dialogue with my wife about a dream? I am sure you know the answer, or you may have several answers, or you might be waiting for my answer. The answer is easy.

Dreams are the manifestation of our deep thoughts, our emotions, our perceptions, our wishes, our hopes, our mysteries, and our disappointments. In brief, they can be anything we feel or do during our daytime or while we are awake and are physically and mentally active. When we dream while we are asleep, we are like actors who are performing on stage after they had memorised the scenario given by the play director. And I carry my occupied country with me everywhere, in my daytime and in my sleep. Just as the Palestinian great poet Mahmoud Darwish said, "My country is a suitcase, and my suitcase is my country."

The accepted truth is everyone dreams in his/her mother tongue, an Arab dreams in Arabic, a French person dreams in French and so on. But when someone dreams in a foreign language, or his/her second language, and not in their mother tongue, this means that this person has become a natural speaker of that language. In other words, he/she has risen to the status of a native speaker of that language. However, for me to achieve that native speaker's status in English, it involved a lot of sacrifice, which included sleepless nights and endless efforts. Yet, some native speaker snobs consider you a near native speaker.

Have you heard the mathematician's dream story? It is said, once upon a time, there was a mathematician that could solve any mathematical problem in the world. But one day, he came across a problem that he could not solve. He spent hours and hours trying to solve it, but he just could not. He felt so frustrated but a mathematician like him would not give up. Therefore, one night he put some blank white paper and a pencil on the table in front of him and began to think. He gazed at the paper for a while, but he felt that his brain was paralysed. Being so exhausted and sleepy, he fell asleep on the blank paper placed on the table.

When he woke up in the morning, he could not believe what he saw on the paper that was blank the night before. He saw that he had filled the page with writing. To his astonishment, he discovered that he had solved the problem in fifty steps while asleep. What a story! I am so poor in mathematics that I always wished I would dream of the exam questions and their solutions. Just like that mathematician, every night I go to bed with one thing in my mind: *my lost country.*

So, are you ready to hear my story with the English language? It is a unique story because I am sure you have never read a book about someone's story, for example, with Russian or Spanish or Arabic.

Let me tell you this, the English language has been my best friend and my bitterest enemy at the same time.

As best friend, it gave me the chance to watch the best TV Channels in the world, and gave me access to limitless number of books, resources, and with the advent of the Internet, English filled my time with knowledge and fun. Above all, English gave me a niche in this world when, at a crucial moment in my life, I was at a crossroad where I had to choose between success and failure, English emerged and took me by hand into its territory and saved my life. English became my only source of living. If I had not learnt English, I would not have been able to raise a family.

By contrast, and I say this with a heavy heart, the English language caused me the greatest suffering that a human being can endure. Being an apprentice in the language for so many years, I suffered from chronic anxiety and stress that would predominate any stage that I had passed through in my attempt to master the language. This made me envious of native speakers who were born with the English tongue, and they had very little to do to master the language. As the proverb goes, "Born with a golden spoon in their mouths." What about me? Was I born with a wooden spoon?

My story with the English language is the story of contradictions: hatred and love, flee or fight, victory, or defeat, surrender or resist, and finally rise from a beginner to a professor to an author. If someone with fair knowledge of the English language had heard me talking in English when I first entered the English language territory, he or she would have laughed to death at the idea that this lousy beginner would be a professor of English, let alone writing books in English one day. What is more, that lousy beginner struggling with his ABC, succeeded in taking the 'Teacher of the Year Award' twice in a span of 20 years. He snatched that award from 150 teachers most of them native English-speaking teachers. That was unthinkable.

This book is the story of rising from fear and anxiety to freedom and victory. It is the story of perseverance and determination to defeat the most powerful language in the world. This book is a lesson of how we should welcome failure because it is the road to success. This book preaches patience, persistence, courage and the belief that 'failure is the foundation of success.' No matter who you are, there is only one motto, 'never give up.' Just as Ray Kroc, acted by (Michael Keaton), the founder of MacDonald's, in the movie the Founder said at the end of the movie, "Persistence is the secret of success."

[1]***"Remember your dreams and fight for them. You must know what you want from life. There is just one thing that makes your dream impossible: the fear of failure."***

– Paulo Coelho, author of Al Chemist, a best seller.

---

[1] Medrut.F. (nd)25 Wise Quotes About Failure (and Coming Back Stronger Than Ever) https://www.goalcast.com/quotes-about-failure/

Chapter 1
My Very First Word in English

As we were climbing the bus steps, my father paused suddenly, touched his top jacket pocket, then turned to me and said, "Ghassoub, run back to the house and get me Al Baibuuk. I think I forgot it in the wooden chest. Hurry up! Faster than wind."

The bus driver, who had one hand on the steering, another on the hand brake, with the engine running, yelled, "Abu Nasir, (my father's nickname) we are late. And you are delaying us." Another passenger from the back shouted, "Yallah, come on Abu Nassir. We want to reach the market while the vegetables and fruit are fresh." Some commented, "Don't waste your time. He has not heard you." My father, who had a serious hearing loss due to his participation in the great war as he used to claim, did not hear any of that, or he pretended, as sometimes others doubted, and just stood at the step waiting for me to come back. My father simply turned his back to the driver, to the passengers and to the whole world.

I, like a gust of wind, ran back into the house, which was not far, rushed to the wooden chest and began searching for that *Al Baibuuk,* but it was not there. My mother, weary of everything, tired and bored, shouted at me to not put the house in a mess because she was sick and exhausted.

I yelled with desperation, almost in tears, "But where is my father's Al Baibuuk? The bus is waiting, and he'll kill me…"

"It is not in the chest. It is in his coat. It is in his coat." She kept repeating.

"But he said it is in the chest," I screamed.

"You, like your father, both are going senile and deaf. It is in his coat. This old man does not remember anything anymore; he is suffering from amnesia. Now shut up and take it from his coat." Then she started moaning, *"Ya waily ya waily…"* What a misery! What a misery!

I was running back to the bus like lightening because I did not want to miss the trip to the city and let alone not to Jerusalem, that had my favourite bazaars and everything there was great and delicious. Besides, to a villager, especially boys in my age, visiting the city was like ascending to heaven. Our village's life was rough and there was an extremely limited choice of everything. All we had a few shops that had sold essentials and very bad quality sweets and candy.

My deepest worry was that my father, with the worst temper in the world, would clash with the bus driver and may get mad and cancel the trip which I had been dreaming of all the week before. Thank God, when I finally returned carrying his Al *Baibuuk*, he was still standing on the bus step.

My father looked at me with his sharp blue eyes flashing that I was late. He snatched the Al *Baibuuk*, inserted it into his inside pocket and climbed the last step. He then paused, pushed his thumb and index finger into his *Kunbaaz* (Palestinian striped gown worn by men) coin pocket, took out some coins, and thrust them into the driver's open palm.

"Abu Nasir. Can't you count today? Give me the full bus fare. You are not a child to pay me half," the driver said angrily. My father ignored what the driver said and just pulled me by my hand, and we took two seats in the middle. The driver swore and yelled but my father did not hear anything, or indeed, did not pay any attention to that. Or he just pretended he did not hear anything as my mother used to say.

"This old man can hear what he likes, and does not hear what he does not like," as she claimed from time to time. Of course, he did not like the driver wanting more money.

As soon as we arrived in Nablus, the second largest city in the West Bank – Palestine, after a bumpy journey on the rough road from the village, something we children enjoyed but was loathed by adults as the bus tossed us up and down, we walked to the Jerusalem's bus station. When I saw the bus, I got excited because it is the kind I preferred, the one we nicknamed in Arabic '*aftas*,' which literally stands for a flattened nose as opposed to a hawked nose '*Abu Booz*,' that has a bonnet.

I loved the *aftas* bus because in the front there is a long seat parallel to the engine and the driver where you can enjoy looking at the road ahead and watch the bus driver at work. Driving a bus in the 1950s was considered like piloting a Jumbo Jet, Boeing 474; and the larger the bus, the more awesome and impressive it is. In retrospect, to me on those days, sitting on that long seat in the front equalled sitting in a Jumbo jet cockpit.

Fearing the bus would depart and my dream journey to Jerusalem would be cancelled that day, I started pulling my father's hand toward the bus shouting, "*Yallah yaba*, come on, Dad, the bus is leaving." We climbed the bus steps, just as the engine was running. My father went to a seat in the middle, and I turned right and sat in the *Jumbo cockpit*.

"Haji,"[2] the bus conductor's voice awakened my father, "the bus fare please."

My father, reluctantly, dipped his thumb, index, and middle finger again for the second time that day into his small pocket and after a while handed the conductor some more coins. But you could tell they were not many. The conductor wearing a funny hat, looked at the money in his palm and yelled, "Haji, this is not enough." Then he looked toward me and asked, "Is that your son there? He has to pay too."

"Yes, he is. He is only seven and is not required to pay. That is all I have. And besides, you are overcharging today. Fear God," my father said with a sharp look at the conductor.

"*Ya khityaar*, Hey old man, I have no time to waste. You either pay the full fare or leave the bus," the conductor said crudely.

My father had bad hearing and the conductor had to repeat several times. But once hearing this, my father lost control of his bad temper and started yelling at the conductor.

"Shame on you. Don't you know who I am? Don't you know who I am? I am a retired officer, an old combatant that was fighting the Jews while you were drinking milk, farting, and shitting in your mother's lap. Are you telling me to get off the bus? Shame on you and your parents who did not raise you properly. Get out of my face before I make you a free show for everyone."

The conductor, whose smile showed that he was not convinced and would not yield to such comedy, told my father to pay and end the story. At that point, my father resorted to his last trick. He pulled his Al *Baibuuk* and started wielding it like a gun telling the conductor to mind what he was saying. That he was addressing a respected army veteran who fought in the great war and served in his majesty's army for 25 years.

---

[2] Haji (a title bestowed on Muslims who had performed the pilgrimage to Mecca, but is used in daily interaction to formally mean Sir or Madam.

In fact, I know my father was a good actor and his techniques worked often and he managed to pay less. Indeed, he seized his right as a war veteran to get a discount on goods and services. But it did not work well all the time.

Voices came from the back telling my father to cut it out as he was delaying the bus. The conductor stunned by my father's outburst was muttering unintelligible words and looked at passengers for support. Finally, the bus moved, and my father won the battle!

After serving 25 years in the army, my father did not get any gratuities or retirement pension money for reasons I did not know. Thus, we did not have a stable income. We were a very small family, only my parents and myself, living in a two-room house built by my father after he left the army. My other three brothers had been living on their own; two were married and joined the army, the third, my second youngest brother had never had a stable job; once a waiter, then a cinema usher, even a manual worker and so on. They had been the only source of money. They had sent money irregularly and the supply trickled to drops and to nothing often. This made us one of the needy families in the village. My father was trying this trick with bus conductors to save some piasters so I could buy things like other boys in Jerusalem.

After that showdown, my father versus the whole world, I decided to show solidarity and sit next to my father. So, I abandoned my seat and sacrificed being the bus co-pilot and joined my father sitting by the window. As I sat, he pinched my thigh, leaned, and whispered into my ear, "You are going to feel rich in Jerusalem. I have saved you two piasters from the claws of those bus' monsters. God damn them. They are greedy and never feel satisfied." I hugged my father and dreamed of buying my favourite sweets from the vendors in Jerusalem. I did not cry at that moment, but now, I cannot stop my tears while writing these words.

In retrospect, if my father had not acted that way, I perhaps would have passed by vendors licking my lips looking with envy at the other children, and sadness filling my heart. My father, the great warrior, the glorious war hero, the battalion commander scarified all this to secure some pence from the paws of the greedy conductors so I could feel like other children.

At the military check point, a soldier mounted the bus with a rifle dangling from his shoulder. He walked along the aisle selecting certain passengers and checking their identities. I wondered why he was doing that and hesitated to ask my father because the soldier could hear us and I might get my father into more trouble. Thus, I kept my mouth shut.

"Can I have your identity card, Haji?" the soldier asked politely.

My father, without hesitation presented his Al Baibuuk, the Red Book, as I saw it. The soldier leafing through it, smiled and returned it to my father saying, "God give you health [3]*yawaldi*," and he passed.

I became very curious about that Red Book and before my father returned it to his pocket with an air of finality, I begged him to let me look at it. He cautioned me to be careful because it was the only Identification he had. I was around seven years old, and I was putting too much pressure on my brain as I was trying to interpret everything around me. In that book, which was the size of a passport, the thing that attracted me most was my father's photo. The man that was sitting next to me wearing Palestinian traditional clothes, looked extremely different in the photo. The only common thing was those sharp blue eyes above the hawked nose, and I was the only one among my brothers that had inherited those eyes.

In that photo, my father was wearing a police uniform of the 1950s and he looked magnificent and confident. I felt so proud. I wondered about that strange hat with a peak at the top and a piece of cloth dangling from the back. Another thing, my father was wearing Hitler's moustache. In the Levant and many other Arab countries, men wore Hitler's moustache because everyone in the Middle East admired him. That was the basis on which I can be accused of antisemitism. But I am not. I hated Hitler once I became mature enough to understand the world.

"Dad, what is this little book?" I asked innocently.

"This was a very important book when I was in the military. At the end of each month when I went to get my salary, the British officer checked this book."

"What is British?"

"Anyone that belongs to Britain. You are Palestinian because you belong to Palestine."

"Can you get any salary now?"

"No. I am not in the military anymore," he whispered.

"Why aren't you in the military?"

He turned his face, looked ahead, and you could tell that question sent him back into history.

---

[3] A formal title of respect said by family and strangers that means my respected father.

"You are still too young to understand." But he never told me, and he died with that question hanging in the air. Why did he leave the army? After 25 years of service, why didn't my father get a pension from the British or the Arab Legion as it was called?

Decades after that exchange with my father and after I became an English teacher myself, to my amusement, that *Al Baibuuk*, the Mysterious Red Book turned out to be a corrupt Arabic pronunciation of 'pay book.' In Arabic, the letter and the sound 'P' does not exist and is replaced by 'B' which can cause confusion and a twist in the meaning. So, Pepsi becomes bebsi and Peter becomes beter. This, indeed, is one of the many difficulties Arab students face while learning English. I laughed as I read the Merriam Webster's definition of **'pay book'** as, '*an individual pay record of a member of the British armed forces.*'

Reminiscing on that event, Al Baibuuk was the first corrupted English word that I had dealt with. This was the beginning of my saga with the English language. Although it was a corrupted form of pay book, I thank my father for teaching me the first word in English.

As we stepped down from the bus, I felt that euphoria that I usually felt whenever I found myself in Jerusalem. We proceeded to the old city entering through the big Bab Al Amood Gate, or Jaffa Gate. Once I entered the old city, I felt transformed into another magic world, similar to my father's tales from the Arabian Nights. Palestinian women, young and old, wearing colourful Palestinian dresses embroidered with thousands beads and colours, sitting on the side of the roads selling farm produce, spices, and eggs and so on. Vendors kept calling passerby to get good deals and literally pulling them by hand to the stalls. "Come on, *Ammi, Haji, waldi*, buy these apples, grapes, figs, they are great for you, fresh from the farm."

The whole city is built with arches and vaults like mosques and churches. Once you are in the old city, the sun becomes invisible, and you have a different feeling. If a child like me had that overwhelming happiness, how about adults who knew some history?

I walked in the roofed souqs and bazaars along the stone streets. They are different from the foot paths and the rough streets in the village. "These streets were made by the Romans 2000 years ago," Dad informed me.

"Dad, who are the Romans?" I asked.

"You will know when you study history at school."

While wading through the crowded narrow streets with my father clutching my hand, I was looking at people and wondering who they were.

However, one group of people looked different from everybody else and attracted my attention. They were taller, with fairer skin and blonde hair, wearing shorts, dark glasses and carrying cameras. Some of the women were very beautiful but they also wore shorts or short skirts and very revealing top wear, sleeveless shirts, and very plunging neckline and so on. And they were walking shoulder to shoulder with Muslim women wearing their garments covering them from top to toe. I noticed they were buying all kinds of things and some boys were running after them trying to sell them something.

"Yaba, dad, who are these people? They look different."

"They are *ingleez,* English tourists."

"They seem to have a lot of money and we have little."

"Yes, they are rich because they make cars, airplanes, canons, and we are still riding donkeys."

"I do not understand their language."

"Of course, they talk ingleezi, English. You will learn English in grade 5. I think."

"Dad. You think if I learn ingleezi, I will be rich like them."

"I think so. But you have to study hard. English is tough. I could not learn a word when I was in the military. But you are still young, and you can learn."

I pulled my father's hand tight several times and pressed my body against his thigh, looking up into his face and said out loud, "Dad. I will learn English and earn a lot of shillings. Then I will give you a lot of piasters and you do not have to bargain with bus conductors."

Hearing that, my father giggled, caressed my cheeks, squatted down, and hugged me saying, "*In shallah, inshallah* if God is willing my son, if God is willing my son. I pray to God to keep me alive to see that day."

I did not cry at that time, but after six decades of that dialogue with my father, I just cannot stop my tears while I am writing these lines now. My father did not live to see that day and he died poor.

Suddenly, we found ourselves out of the crowd onto another less crowded street under the shining sun and my father tapped my shoulder and said, "Now you are walking on the *Path of Suffering* (Via Dolorosa)."

"What's that?" I asked.

"According to the Christian faith, it is the path where Christ, *peace be upon him*, walked to be crucified. But in Islam we have a different version."

Although I did not understand very much, I kept quiet. Then we walked into a big yard where I could see many of the ingleezi tourists who were going in and coming out of a big gate in the corner and many as well standing in that yard.

"Why are there many Ingleezi here?" I asked and shook my father's hand for an answer.

"Here is the Church of Holy Sepulcher, the holiest place for all Christians. They claim that Jesus was crucified and buried here."

"Please, Dad. Let us visit."

"Inshallah, if God wills, we will go in in our next visit to Jerusalem. But now it is time for Friday's prayer. Let's go to the Al Aqsa Mosque."

This mosque is the third holiest site in Islam. It was customary for my father to perform his Friday prayer there whenever he had some money. I was his companion in those trips.

With hindsight, when I think of my father's reaction to my request to enter the church, he simply promised to visit the church on our next visit to Jerusalem. He did not mention anything negative about Christianity or tell me to shut up. Instead, he was very relaxed and said the time was late for such a visit. What is more, my father kept his promise and took me into the Holy Sepulcher on our next visit.

The church looked a bit scary from the inside with its statues and paintings, and the priests wearing black from head to toe and chains dangling from their necks. I kept asking questions and my father was trying his best to clarify and give me whatever information he had to satisfy my little inquisitive mind. One of the priests put his hand on my head and asked me about my age and exchanged some words with my father about tourists and so on. What surprised me was that the priest was Palestinian and spoke Arabic. It was not the only visit; I also visited the Holy Sepulcher with my eldest brother in the years to come.

Now, when I reflect on that, I know that I was given my first lesson in tolerance and how we should accept other religions and other cultures at a young age.

On another occasion while we were entering the Dome of the Rock, the holy shrine of the cave where the Prophet Muhammed, *peace be upon him*, stopped on his Night Journey from Mecca before his ascension into heaven, I had another encounter with the English language. As I entered the shrine, I saw a well-dressed man who looked Palestinian, surrounded by some ingleezi, and he was talking loudly to them in ingleezi, English. I stood and wondered what he was saying. They were standing like school children listening to this man very attentively. That fascinated me and coined in my little mind a secret. "If you speak English, you captivate people."

"He is a tourist guide," my father interrupted my thought.

"What's a tourist guide?"

"Someone from the country who speaks good English so he can explain to the tourists about what they see and answer their questions."

"Does he make a lot of money?"

"Oh yes. He gets a good salary maybe, and these rich tourists will give him a good *bakhsheesh*, tip as well."

"Dad, I want to study English when I grow up. I do not want to enter the army like my brother," I said excitedly.

He said, "I pray to see that day when you are a big man in English. God willing."

Chapter 2
The English Woman in a Bikini at the Dead Sea

The first time I had encountered authentic English language in my life was on my first trip ever to the Dead Sea which was around 80 km from the village. I was around 9:00 at the time. My second youngest brother, who was working as a waiter at the Dead Sea Hotel, had consistently refused to take me there and turned a deaf ear to my pleas and nagging.

But I did not give up. One day, I formed a diabolic plan in my head. One evening, while my brother was spending his leave with us, I started pleading while my mother was present so I could arouse her anger. And the plan worked.

"If you don't take this boy to this what you call…what? Yes. Dead Sea, this boy might die, and the crime will tighten around your neck until the Day of Judgement," she said angrily. No one could say No to Mom who had a temper. My mother, who had never seen a sea or a river or any stretch of water, wondered, "God damn it! Why do they call it this…you know…dead?"

"I told you mom a hundred times. Fish cannot live there," my brother answered.

"Okay, okay. Who cares? Just take this boy there and make sure he does not die in that thing…I don't know."

"Yama. This boy is an unrefined *Fallaah*, real peasant, has never left the village, and he will act awkwardly among city people and hotel staff. Besides his funny village accent is disgraceful. Worse than that, he cannot use a fork and a knife and when he starts licking his fingers, gobbling food like a donkey, and eating noisily, he will scandalise me among my colleagues at the hotel and civilized tourists. I don't want to be the laughingstock of the Dead Sea community."

"Okay. Then teach him all that etiquette. God Knows you were using your feet to eat before you called yourself civilized." She paused and added, "Teach him all that. Just shut up and take your brother. Make sure he does not die in that...what you call...I forgot."

"The Dead Sea, Mom, the Dead Sea Mom."

[4]"*Toz.*"

Finally, my brother agreed to take me but warned me to obey his instructions or otherwise smacks would fall on my face.

"I will kick your arse if you wag your tail at me. You know," he warned me while mother had turned her back. I jumped in the air. I had never felt such euphoria in my life. I dashed to mother, who had poor health, kissed her cheeks and her hands. I hugged her as she was pushing me saying, "You little genie, stop or you will kill me."

That night, I could not sleep and was counting the seconds to start my first trip to the sea. I had never seen a sea before. Besides, it meant a long ride in the bus, which was also joyful. So, you can imagine the excitement. I told all my classmates and peers and spread the big news. I know they were eating their hearts out with jealousy.

The following day, I mounted the taxi while my peers were standing by filled with envy. I think I was the first boy in that era of our village to visit the Dead Sea, or any sea. I felt proud and I looked at my friends from the taxi windows with my eyes twinkling with delight and contempt for them. They made faces at me and stuck their tongues out, and, of course, I did retaliate.

As the bus began to approach the Dead Sea, I began to feel excited. This would be the first time in the life of a peasant boy from a hilly village hidden by the olive groves to see the sea. Before this trip, the biggest stretch of water I had seen did not exceed one to three meters of rainwater gathered in the fields in pools. The sight of water in winter pools always fascinated us and we spared no opportunity to take off our clothes and jump in those pools to swim. The village had no water spring or water tanks, and the only source of water was the collected rainwater in water wells dug by villagers. Once, I got excited and jumped into a pool in spring to find myself stuck in mud and dirt.

As soon as I saw that huge blue stretch of blue water, I shouted, "*Ya Yama, Ya Yaba*, (Oh Mom, oh Dad) what is this. Look! The sea. The sea!" I began to jump on my seat and the other passengers laughed and giggled. My brother was

---

[4] a word from the Levant's Arabic slang which shows indifference like 'who cares.'

pressing my hand and was telling me to calm down. He turned to the couple sitting in the seat behind and said, "I am sorry. My brother is a peasant, and he has never been to a beach before. Excuse us. He cannot hide his excitement." The couple said they did not mind, and that they thought the boy looked gorgeous. Then I squeezed my brother's hand and shook him asking, "Brother. I am amazed. Why does the sea water look blue? It is different from the water in the village which sometimes looks brown."

"I am not sure. Maybe because of the sky. The sky is blue, and the sea reflects that colour. I don't know," my brother said.

I just found that scene dazzling. Besides, the Dead Sea had a special smell. The scene was a mixture of a very hot sun, salty sea, and mirage.

When we arrived at the hotel, we went to the staff quarter and my brother accommodated me in his room on an additional bed that he requested. I said, "Brother. I would like to stay at the hotel."

"That is for tourists and guests. It is not for us. You will have to work all your life to save to spend one night there."

I shut up.

Later, I received my first table etiquette lesson. My brother seated me in the staff's canteen, placed a napkin on my lap, and started teaching me how to use a knife and a fork.

"Remember. Rule number 1: the knife is in the right hand, and the fork is in the left." Next, he showed me how to cut the piece of chicken. I thought that was easy, but once I tried, I found it too difficult. Then two of his colleagues joined and he introduced me. They kissed me and said, "This boy is good looking, and he will have a bright future."

One shouted, "Where did you get those blue eyes boy? Are you British or Danish or what?" Everyone laughed. It seemed that my brother was so popular among his colleagues for his great sense of humour.

As they chatted, I struggled with the damn fork and knife, but I had no success. I was scared of my brother, but I was starving. I ended up holding the piece of chicken in my hand and my brother's eyes burned with anger, but he could not do anything as he was surrounded by others. And I knew how to take advantage of that moment. The food was so delicious, out of this world.

Now I wanted to swim in the Dead Sea, and I was nagging to the point that I looked like a bull charging on a matador, as my brother described the scene decades later. Before we went to swim, my brother held my hand, warning me that the Dead Sea water is extremely salty.

"Stay with me, do not let the water go into your mouth or your eyes. Especially your eyes; they will burn like hell, and you will be blind for some time. The Dead Sea has no mercy. Understand? It will make you vomit." I shook my head.

"I know you are as stubborn as a bull. This is because of the cow's milk I used to steal for you from the neighbour's farm when you were a baby." I laughed and so did he. I loved that brother the most.

"One more thing. Here in the Dead Sea, anything floats. Just keep water away from your mouth and your eyes."

That was my first theoretical lesson in swimming. But in my excitement, I was not listening to all that and I was fixated on how I would jump into that blue water. As we were walking toward the beach from the staff quarters, I was pulling my brother like a dog that had been inside for days and now it is trying to free itself from the leash. And that is what happened. I broke the leash and ran to the water, and I could hear my brother shouting, but I just dived into the water. *No one can dive into the Dead Sea unless you are a peasant from a hilly village in Palestine.*

There I suffered my worst shock in my whole life. When my brother laid me on the beach, he was rubbing my eyes with fresh water. My eyes were burning so much I felt blind. I was vomiting because of that salty water I had swallowed. I thought I was going to die. I could hear my brother and his friends laughing. "You peasant son of a peasant," I could hear one of them saying. "Boy, this is not a village rainwater pool. This is the Dead Sea. No compromise. Luckily, you did not die. Your luck splits the rock (*an Arabic saying which means you are very lucky*)." He pinched my rosy cheek, and everyone giggled. I learnt the lesson well: Do not jump into water until you know what kind of water it is.

As I sat on the beach recovering from that shock, sipping some drinking water, rinsing my mouth continuously, rubbing my burning eyes fiercely, my vision began to return slowly after a temporary blindness. My brother who was sitting next to me rubbing me with a towel was saying, "You see. Mother said do not die here. If you want to die, go to that high oak tree in the village and jump."

I nodded and admitted my stubbornness and stupidity for not taking his instructions seriously, and he said as if inflicting vengeance on me, "The Dead

Sea knew you were guilty and you did not obey your brother, so he punished you." I looked horrified. A seven-year-old boy could believe such a myth.

"Do you know that this Dead Sea had swallowed two cities in the ancient times because the people were wicked and disobeyed God? When you grow older, you will learn about Sodom and Gomorrah at school."

As I was listening to my brother, my vision had already returned to me, and I began to see and hear what was going around me on the beach. This was the first time in my life to sit on a beach and watch how life was so different from life in the hilly village there in the middle of Palestine. I watched people swimming, walking, and children running and shouting.

But something fascinated me. While I was gazing at that thing, I pressed my brother's shoulder hard and repeatedly and said pointing at that thing, "Brother. Oh. Look. Look. There are some naked women there. They will go to hell."

My brother laughed and said, "You primitive peasant, they are not naked; they are wearing bikinis."

"Wearing what?"

"Bikini. Bikini."

"What is that?"

"A swimming suit."

"But they will go to hell. God will put them in the fire because they are wearing nothing."

"Yes, they are wearing something. They are wearing bikinis."

"Do you call that something." I protested. "If my mother saw them, she would chase them with her stick."

"Thank God your mother is not here. Shut up and leave those English tourists alone. Today is not the Judgement Day. Now come to swim and I'll teach you how to handle the Dead Sea. You have already learnt Rule One and received punishment for breaking that, Rule: NEVER JUMP OR DIVE INTO THE DEAD SEA." Then he added, "Just wade your way into the water as if you are stepping on hot ashes."

Despite that tough experience with the Dead Sea in my first crazy jump, I and the salty sea became friends. I spent two weeks there and I enjoyed myself thoroughly. I made progress on all fronts; table etiquette, swimming, and above all suppressing my excitement so I did not scandalise my brother with my primitive behaviour. But one thing I longed to do, I wished I could speak *Ingleezi*, English, so I could talk to those beautiful women in bikinis.

Between me and myself, I argued that that so called bikini covered so little and they, compared to my mother and girls in the village who were covered from top to toe, were naked. I yearned to talk to those beautiful women who looked like mermaids just emerged from the sea. But alas, my English did not exceed 'hello' and some words that my brother had taught me.

One early evening as I was strolling along the beach collecting shells to take back to the village as a proof to my friends that I had visited the Dead Sea and to get them to boil with envy, I came very close to the front of the hotel. My brother, who was serving a group of people, called me, and signalled to me to come over. He introduced me to them in English, but I could not reply to any question they asked.

One lady wearing a bikini said something and my brother translated that she thought I was gorgeous and with my blue eyes, I looked somehow English. She gave me two shillings which was a big amount of money those days. I blushed and tried to refuse the money because that would be disgraceful, but I could not resist that offer. The two shillings would provide pocket money in the village for a month or more! I looked at my brother and he said nothing.

The next day, I saw the lady who gave me the shillings and we swam together. She recognised me and said, "Hi, English boy." I blushed and kept quiet.

As we sat on the beach, she tried to teach me some English. "My name is Charlotte."

Then she pointed at me and I parroted, "My name is Ghassoub."

"I come from England."

"I come from…" I hesitated because I did not how to say *Filisteen* in English. "Palestine…Palestine." She repeated slowly.

I kept repeating after her and I was doing very well. She wrote on the sand sometimes. She told my brother later that I had the right aptitude for English, and I would make a perfect English gentleman in the future. My brother and his colleagues and other staff wondered how a nine-year-old boy could strike up friendship with such a beautiful lady, while they had never been able to do that. They started calling me a Palestinian star.

After almost six decades from that unexpected incident in the beginning of my life and with hindsight, my first lesson in English had been conducted by a native speaker from the heart of Britain, and without any previous planning.

Charlotte was a great teacher; she used the best method an English teacher can think of. She would point at herself and say, "I am Charlotte. I am from England."

Then I would do the same. "I am Ghassoub, I am from Palestine," I repeated and repeated.

She, then, would point toward the sea and make me repeat loud, "Sea, beach, swimming," and so on. Charlotte's very affectionate nature caused all my hesitation and shyness to melt away to be replaced by courage.

She was so amused when I started acting while repeating words such as standing, walking, as if I had been acting in a movie. I even tried to mimic her accent which made her laugh heartily. I was having a good time and enjoying myself. I felt Charlotte was like a sister, something I had been deprived of, spoiling her good-looking younger brother. In fact, to a passerby, we looked closely related considering the similarity in physical features.

From a second or first language acquisition point of view, I represented the critical age hypothesis which states that the younger the learner is, the more adaptable he or she is for acquiring a language. Although there has been a long-standing debate among linguists concerning this theory, I have concluded through my long teaching career that it is true to say that the younger the person is, the easier it is for him or her to acquire a language.

Although Charlotte was not an English teacher, unconsciously she was using the Direct Method in teaching. If you do not know what the Direct Method in language teaching is, let me tell you something. It is one of the many approaches to language teaching in which the teacher engages the learners in the session and teaches everything through the target language without using one single word from the learners' mother tongue.

Charlotte was so friendly, sympathetic, funny, patient and interested in people that if I had been 27 years old at the time, there would have been a love story between a Palestinian and a British girl. After two weeks, I returned to the village among the hills with a collection of tales to a joyous welcome from my friends, neighbours and my parents. The boys would gather around me under the olive tree and listen passionately to my endless stories and adventures by the Dead Sea. They gasped at my reckless plunge into the Killer Sea and marvelled at the possibility of the Dead Sea swallowing me like the two cities.

But my encounter with the lady in a bikini thrilled them the most and it proved too hard to get them to listen as they could not control their excitement.

They could not imagine how pretty she was. I would ask about the prettiest girl in the village, and they would name many, but none would match Charlotte's beauty.

Then I said, "This girl you have just named, the beauty of the village as you claim, has one fraction of Charlotte's." This sent them into a frenzy. Even one or two plunged to the ground spinning on their backs like donkeys taking a dust bath. When I reflect on this now, if my peers listened to the teacher's explanation the way they had listened to my stories, they would have earned full marks in their tests.

"Did you kiss her?" one shouted.

But the most impressive invisible commodity I had brought to the village was the English words and phrases I had stored in my memory. My friends begged me to teach them, and they would start mimicking like parrots. My father in particular felt proud, and he would say, "Talk to your uncle in English." Then I would look at the old man and say, "Hi, how are you? My name is Ghassoub." I would sometimes stutter, hesitate, forget, scratch my head, act foolishly, and pretend I am an English boy. I was good at acting from an early age and that quality made me more admirable.

The old men watching this performance used to raise their hands and exclaim, "*Mashaallah*, God's great. This boy is talking *ingleezi*. God protect him."

In fact, one of the beliefs in our culture in that era was that 'those who manage to master the English language were seen as geniuses and extraordinary people.'

"He is now a real English cub. Isn't he?" my mother was heard saying. She sometimes looked at me while sipping tea with her mates, her eyes full of love, and said, "Look at him. Isn't he an admirable English cub?" With hindsight, I think my mother's frequent repetition of describing me as an English cub was a good omen according to the superstition of those days.

Did the Dead Sea give me a new life by not submerging me like Sodom and Gomorrah? Yes, it did. It pushed me to the surface, and I emerged like [5]Atlantis to start a new life. But my encounter with Charlotte made me love everything British. She was nice to me, and this made me love the English language and I excused her for wearing a bikini because I concluded that was her business.

---

[5] According to Greek mythology, Atlantis was submerged into the Atlantic Ocean by God.

Although the British were hated for giving Palestine to the Jews, Charlotte's sympathy, patience, and generosity toward me made me forget the bad things that the British did to us.

Unfortunately, that would be the last time I would have the chance to have a holiday near the Dead Sea. That trip to the Dead Sea was the dream of every boy and girl of my age in the village. Did the Dead Sea trip contribute to shaping my future? I think it did. The encounter with Charlotte was a major milestone on my life journey's passage. Although I was nine years old going on ten, I began to dream of becoming an English teacher or anything to do with English.

Before the Dead Sea trip, whenever anyone had asked me about what I wanted to be in the future, I always answered that I wanted to be an army officer like my eldest brother, then I would jump and salute. But after the Dead Sea trip, the dream to be an army officer had vanished to be replaced by the dream to be an English teacher, or as Charlotte said, an English gentleman.

After joining the military boarding secondary school and becoming a young man, my trips to the Dead Sea became like a pilgrimage to honour my brother's and Charlotte's memory. I would sit on the beach gazing into the horizon and reminiscing about those beautiful adventures of my childhood. The events passed through my mind like a movie, first, jumping into the Dead Sea and how I got myself blinded and choked by the saltiest water in the world. This was like jumping into the hot lava of a volcano. Second, Charlotte teaching me English and spoiling me like her young brother. Third, my outraged brother training me dinner etiquette, and his constant yelling at me: you are a peasant, son of a peasant, and you will never be civilized.

The Dead Sea episode, although short, was one of the most important episodes that shaped my life. In that short episode of my early life, I learned things that impacted me for decades to come. As my father used to say, "Learning at a young age is like carving in stone." Looking back at that crucial stage of my life, I concluded that if this had not happened or I had not met Charlotte, I might be either the [6]Unknown Soldier or a retired army officer now, and there would have never been a book titled *My English Language Journey*.

---

[6] An unidentified soldier killed in war, given burial with special honors in a national memorial.

Chapter 3
Learning My ABC

It's the year 1960, I am in grade 5, I am now in class and today I begin learning English at school as a second language. I have been waiting for this moment since I left the Dead Sea, around two years ago. It is my first English lesson at school. We are 40 pupils in the classroom, and we are waiting for the English teacher impatiently which is something unusual for pupils, who are typically so bored with school, to be waiting for a teacher impatiently! We are wondering what he is going to teach us. One boy says, "I pray to God that we are not going to memorise anything like Arabic poetry." I yell at the boys that English is mine, I learnt English a long time ago, and they know no English. I can teach but I do not want to.

"If I teach you, you will take my smartness and I will end up nothing." That was a fallacy among us, and we tended not to cooperate very much because of that myth. One boy tells me to stop showing off and keep my English to myself because the teacher is coming, and he will teach English for free.

When the teacher enters, the noise dies down and we stand up. Silence prevails and we are full of expectations and attention. I pray that the teacher asks about something I know, something from the Dead Sea, something Charlotte had already taught me. So, I can show off and the boys feel jealous. The teacher, Mr. Waleed, a young man from the village, stood in the front, wearing a tie and a suit, and he was smiling. Yes, I said, he was smiling. Teachers those days rarely smiled because frowning was one of their weapons to scare us which was necessary to keep discipline. "Don't give those young devils a chance, or your class will be lentil soup (*an Arabic proverb for a chaotic situation*)." That was the conventional wisdom those days. But this teacher is smiling and is not carrying a cane or a stick.

A teacher is smiling, really! A teacher in that era did not smile. Teachers had iron faces, ruled with an iron fist, but because they could not carry an iron stick or bars, they carried wooden sticks. Most men in the village carried sticks for different purposes, for self-defence perhaps, and that was a common sight. However, the only two groups of people that carried sticks to punish others were shepherds and teachers.

But this teacher, contrary to the norms of those days, did not carry a stick either, instead he carried a long roll of paper which had a kind of a wooden stick at the centre. We wondered what that was. We thought this teacher had brought a more sophisticated stick to enjoy torture more. Mr. Waleed looked at the class and said his first phrase in English, "Good morning, boys," and with a gesture from his hand encouraging us to repeat, there was sporadic reaction; some giggled, some repeated, some kept their mouths shut and looked puzzled, but I was one of the few who replied very loud and with gusto.

Next, Mr. Waleed moved to the blackboard, and we thought as usual, he was going to write the day, the date, etc. Instead, he unrolled the big roll he was carrying and hung it on the blackboard. Once the roll was in full view, I could not believe my eyes, I rubbed my eyes twice, focused more, and because I sat in the front, I had the best view of what was going on in the front. I thought God had listened to my prayer because that poster depicted a view of a beach in the summer, a different world which I was familiar with but most of the other boys were not. It looked almost the same as the Dead Sea beach, but, luckily, it was a drawing, otherwise, the sight of real bikinis would have distracted us as we were on the threshold of adolescence.

As soon as the teacher had fixed the poster on the wall, I could not suppress my excitement and involuntarily, I sprang to my feet, pointing my index finger in the air, forgetting the number one rule of the classroom strict etiquette; *raise your hand and talk when given permission*, and shouted, "Beach…this beach. *Ustath*, (Arabic word for master). this beach." The Master turned toward the voice source and looked at me. Silence fell on the room, and the boys, most of them sadists, waited to see how this new teacher would react to an offender. They thought, as they told me later, that I had just stupidly offered myself to test the intensity of this teacher's smacks and kicks because he did not carry a stick, which would have been a free show for them.

Instead, Mr. Waleed broke the silence, raised his hands in the air in approval shouting in both English and Arabic, "Well done, boy. Give him a hand, boys."

A loud applause followed, I felt flattered, and looked at the boys triumphantly. I was the star of that session because Mr. Waleed praised me frequently as I answered most questions, and I was on my feet most of the time. But the most exciting moment for me was when the teacher pointed to the lady wearing a bikini eliciting any answer about her, and I screamed, "Sir…Sir…Bikini…bikini." Most of the boys burst out laughing at the sound of the word because they did not know what I was talking about.

That session was a hive of activities and entirely different from the other sessions. Traditionally, teachers had been concerned with discipline, blind obedience, memorisation, and their sessions looked like a hot dog factory. However, Mr. Waleed's session gave students freedom to move, act, and talk, go to the blackboard, without many restrictions. Perhaps, for the first time, the boys felt they were in some control of their learning. They looked happy, they enjoyed the session, they did not feel bored and did not wait for the bell impatiently as in the other boring Total-Teacher-Controlled-Sessions (TTCS).

What's more, our homework was to draw a beach from memory on a piece of paper so in the coming session, you can tell the class about the beach in English as much as you can. That was a real novelty and contrary to the norms where the session ends by the teacher demanding that that passage or that poem should be memorised, or be copied five times, or you will face the stick.

We went home so excited. This teacher is different. And I became the authority on the English language for most boys in my class who begged me for help with their homework and even they bribed me with fruit from their farms and sweets made by their mothers. I dreamed of Charlotte most of the time and wondered where she was to see all this.

During the session, Mr. Waleed made us sing the alphabet bit by bit so we could memorise the first six or seven letters or more, which was easy. This made the session more enjoyable as the teacher made us sing those letters in chorus from time to time. With hindsight, Mr. Waleed made us sing the ABC for a purpose. He knew if our parents asked us, "What did you learn at school today?" Our answer would be singing some of the English alphabet and that would keep them satisfied. The other tradition that generations had observed on those days was that when pupils learnt the English alphabet for the first time, they would rush out of school at the end of school day racing in the village's roads and narrow alleyways singing the English alphabet at the top of their voices and announcing to the world, *"Now I know my ABC."*

In Palestine, and my village in particular, education and earning a qualification has been as important as food. Although many fathers needed their children desperately on those days to help them in the farms, no single boy according to my vivid memory had been withdrawn from school. When mothers sent their children to school in the morning, they would raise their hands toward heavens and pray, "God! Let me live to the day when my child comes back carrying his certificate so I can sing and hang it on the wall so the whole world can see it."

Reflecting on that very first English session that took place almost five decades ago, I find myself fascinated by Mr. Waleed's approach. Being an English teacher for more than four decades myself, having taught English to all levels from beginners to advanced myself, having observed many colleagues in the classroom and having been observed so many times, I can judge Mr. Waleed's session as one of the best I have seen. How Mr. Waleed deviated from the norms in that era where the translation method was predominant and the sole objective of the session was to teach a list of words and some grammatical rules through Arabic, is still a mystery to me?

Although he practiced teaching English in the 1960s, Mr. Waleed had employed very modern strategies in teaching English. He did not use a particular method known to English teachers as the Direct Method, or the Translation method, or the Aural-Oral approach, and so on, he, in fact, employed a combination of these methods. He had cleverly taken some elements from everything and created a great recipe for an exciting session. In that session, he was a behaviourist, a constructivist and structuralist. Above all, he was acting within the communicative language teaching approach. "*Communicative Language Teaching (CLT)…emphasises interaction as both the means and the ultimate goal of learning a language.*" (Rahmi, 2009)

Obviously, his objective was to teach English as a means of communication rather than a school subject to take exams. Basically, his sole intention was to give every pupil the chance to participate, and he managed to engage everyone in the lesson. Mr. Waleed's session was full of interaction and was conducted in both the target language and sometimes the pupils' native tongue. He took advantage of Arabic, the pupils' native tongue, to give instructions and to direct action. That saved so much time as Arabic was used as an instrument to enhance learning. After all, using the learners' mother tongue occasionally in teaching a foreign language is an added advantage that non-native teachers of English possess.

The pupils were allowed to move freely sometimes; they even rushed to the poster and challenged each other to guess what this and that was. In contrast, in other classes, we were not allowed to even twitch our eyelids. When I think about that now, I conclude that some controlled chaos can teach effectively, while too much discipline can ruin the atmosphere. For the first time, the pupils including myself arrived home telling their families how enjoyable their first English class was. I, of course, reiterated to my parents my intention to become an English teacher like Mr. Waleed. Until that moment, Charlotte and Mr. Waleed had played a major role in shaping my destiny to become an English teacher.

Grade 5 was an exciting journey into English led by Mr. Waleed as he managed skilfully to teach us to communicate in English and at the same time to prepare us for the grammar and vocabulary exams that had been prescribed by the curriculum. If he had not done that, he would have been accused of deviating from the syllabus and would have received a warning letter from the principal. On those days, everyone—school administration, parents, shepherds, even sheep were interested in marks only. Your grade report is the only thing that counted. You could have given your father a presentation on Shakespeare in pure English, but if your grade was not B or A, you would be doomed a failure.

When we moved to grade 6, Mr. Zaidan, the English teacher was not interested in anything called communicative, his main obsession was to teach bilingual vocabulary lists and grammatical rules. Worse than that, most of the session interaction was done in Arabic and only a little fraction in English. He was heavily engaged in the Grammar Translation method and seemed to despise Mr. Waleed's communicative approach or mixed approach. Again, we fell into the abyss of TTCS, Besides, the pupils were not encouraged to talk but to memorise words.

Grade 6 in Jordan's school system marked the end of the primary stage. I was 13 years old and eligible to go into the intermediate stage. My total English repertoire consisted of ABC, some English words, some grammatical rules, and the ability to read at a very basic level. But the biggest wealth I had was the motivation to learn English created by Mr. Waleed, whose memory is still vivid in my head, and the love for English and for the English people and their culture created by Charlotte of the Dead Sea.

But the most important thing I had gained was '*the courage to interact orally without worrying about mistakes.*' This may sound contradictory; how can making mistakes be considered an ability or a skill? The answer is that if you can communicate in a foreign language with mistakes and you can convey the message confidently, this indicates that you are not suffering from '*language anxiety*', which in my opinion as a second language learning and teaching expert, is one of the biggest obstacles toward learning a second language. Language anxiety is the fear of making mistakes which can be so intense that it prevents students especially adults from speaking in public.

This unpleasant feeling causes the individual to avoid talking in the target language in the classroom or in other situations to save face. So, you can imagine how language anxiety can impact negatively on language learning. Those students who suffer from this phenomenon do not participate in language sessions and even become aloof and unsociable in their daily life. I have met a lot of them in my career as a language teacher.

Let me tell you about my experience with language anxiety. When I was learning English at university as a major, in my second year something happened that made me challenge the English language more and more. One day, as I and some other students were sitting in a circle in a professor's house talking and discussing various topics, that professor with the name Douglas turned to me and asked me directly, "Mustafa," using my family name, "what do you think of the Palestinian Israeli conflict?" All the eyes of the six or seven students turned to me. I did not feel nervous, but as I adjusted my seat and was getting ready for lecturing, someone in the circle said something shocking that caused tension in the atmosphere and made me pause for a while.

That person said as I was preparing to talk, "Let's count the mistakes." That person was one of my Palestinian friends, but he was narcissistic. Do you know what a narcissistic person is? It is someone who admires himself/herself excessively to the point that he or she thinks he or she is the best looking and the best in everything in the world that no one can match their beauty, or their elegance or their intelligence. If you want to know the origins of this term, read the Greek Legend of Narcissus. I know that narcissistic friend felt so jealous because the professor directed that question at me and not at him because he always wanted to show off and be the centre of attention. And by saying that, he was planning to silence me so he could take the stage. But his plan failed because the professor said to him straight in the face, "Mustafa is one of the best speakers in the English Department." Then he turned to me and said, "We are all ears, Mustafa."

This daring counterattack by the professor on my narcissistic friend boosted my confidence and my assertiveness and that friend continued to boil with indignation. I thanked the professor and ended my long probing gaze at that friend. He responded by giving a sheepish laugh and I was sure he felt embarrassed and ashamed of what he said. Having regained control of my self-confidence, I launched into answering that big question with great enthusiasm as if nothing had happened. But honestly, I do not remember if I had made any mistakes because that narcissistic friend never handed me a list of my mistakes. All I remember was that I was asked many questions at the end of my talk. That friend was struck dumb silent.

With hindsight, if I had had language anxiety, that comment made by my narcissistic friend would have devastated me and left me to submit to despair. Instead, it sharpened my enthusiasm and energy to achieve greatness in English. That day, I took an oath to work day and night to perfect my English and to reach the highest level of fluency and accuracy I could. As a result, in a matter of months, I left that narcissistic friend speechless whenever he had the chance to hear me talking in English in or outside class because there were no mistakes to count. And what angered him more was that I had never tried to open the matter with him. But as Buddha said, "The best form of revenge is improvement." That is true.

In our life, we must learn lessons from mistakes and situations we go through. That incident in my long and turbulent journey in the English language taught me several invaluable lessons. First, do not react to criticism and do not retaliate, but respond by acting. And do not carve insults on stone but write them on sand so the wind will blow them off. Third, I swore that day when I become a teacher of English, I will be so cautious when I criticise my low performing students and give them encouraging comments rather than harsh words that hurt their feelings. I do not want any of my students to feel the embarrassment and shame that I felt that day when that jealous and narcissistic friend made his ridiculous comment in front of the professor and classmates.

Chapter 4
Oliver Twist of Jordan

My mother's death at the end of my primary stage of schooling marked a major turning point in my personal history. This was the most tragic event of my life. It had sent me into my partial exile that I called my first diaspora because the second diaspora, the loss of my country, followed suit three years later. No one can choose when to die, but my mother, who had spent the last decade of her life struggling between poor health and the responsibility of looking after my father and raising me, always anticipated an early death. She died in her 50s, if I remember correctly.

I remember her daily supplication raising her hands toward heavens pleading, "Ya Allah – My God, I am not greedy or asking for a lot, all I want is to lend me more time in this life to raise this boy so he can stand on his feet because no one will look after him when I depart." Indeed, if she had departed some years earlier, my destiny, perhaps, would have changed for the worse and I would not be what I am now.

After my mother's death, my eldest brother, a lieutenant in the army who had good connections with some high-ranking officers, secured me a place in a military boarding school in Amman. The school was under the control of the educational department in the military forces but followed the Ministry of Education curriculum. The only one of its type in Jordan. It was mainly for *Martyrs' Sons*, and for tribal boys whose folk still lived a nomadic life.

The school consisted of the last two stages of schooling, the preparatory stage, and the secondary stage. Each consisted of three years. We were fully responsible for our daily life and hygiene. The school provided us with a quasi-military uniform and a wooden chest to store our belongings. If you did not have a good lock on that chest, the boys would steal everything.

The canteen or mess hall, as we referred to it those days – terms left by the British military that mandated Jordan until 1946 – provided three meals. Students received a little amount of food, so they rarely left the mess hall full, but always still hungry. For this reason, some students attempted to get more food which often ended in failure. The cooks simply refused to serve more food and they justified their action by claiming that these were the seniors' orders, besides, that was the ration.

"I am as a slave, and I follow orders. If you are not happy with your ration, you can go and complain to his Excellency the school's principal," the cook usually said.

The situation in the canteen when a boy attempted to get more food, ended in one of three outcomes. One, the cooks would, after hesitation and some words of rebuke, give some little amount to save face and get rid of the beggar. The second, the cooks would refuse to give any extra food and the boy returns to his stone seat with head down, humiliated, and other boys laughing at him and calling him coward and other derogatory names. The third scenario, which was the most exciting, a battle between the boy and the cooks resulted, and the boys in the canteen start cheering as if they were in a Roman theatre watching gladiators massacring each other. The boy 'asking for more' with all eyes on him and the boys urging him to fight, raises his voice, and a verbal battle with the two cooks starts. In some cases, he throws his mess kit at them, and they retaliate by using their long ladles trying to hit him. But because cooks were separated by a wall in their booth, a fist fight never took place. In some cases, the boy retreats to his seat feeling defeated, or rushes out, and in other cases, the boy is escorted by the teacher on duty to spend some time in detention.

Our life in the boarding school was coloured with many fights where sometimes the boys hurt each other badly and the case escalated, which might involve two gangs. Boredom, lack of activities, living in a kind of concentration camp, led to fights among the boys. As fighting erupted, the boys would make a circle and watch the wrestling just like movies, but there was no betting.

However, fighting with the cooks in the canteen was the most popular as the cooks were seen as enemies of the poor people because they refused to give more food than the ration. The boys aged 12-20, according to popular belief required three times the amount of ration they had been given. School officials, aware of this fact, did nothing. Actually, the boys scraped their plates with their spoons so that they did not need washing. Then when they left the mess hall, the stone tables did not need clearance because apart from breadcrumbs, the tables were clean. Most boys tried to sneak out of the camp to buy some food from the shops in the neighbourhood if they had money.

But what has learning English to do with our mess hall and starvation among students? Our English course material, in every level, from first preparatory to 3rd secondary, the last stage, consisted of a textbook, possibly a workbook, and a story. The textbook contained reading comprehension passages that were followed by a multitude of exercises such as comprehension questions, filling gaps, and so on. The reading passages, mostly extracted from English literature, were very boring for several reasons. First, the passages were very hard for the students as they were full of new words, and the teacher had to translate almost every word into Arabic. As the boys wrote the meanings and sometimes the pronunciation in Arabic, the page looked horrible as the English text had almost disappeared under the heavy notes in Arabic.

The second reason for not understanding the passages was the cultural aspect of the passage. For example, the passages contained information about British culture which was hard to understand as the students had no background knowledge and a completely different lifestyle. In addition, the students, of course, struggled with the difficult vocabulary. The only motivation they had was exam anxiety. They, of course, feared failure and they had to pay some attention to pass the exam. English was taught just like any other subject and not as a means of communication. Mr. Waleed's and Charlotte's days had gone with the wind.

However, one day, one reading passage changed that monotony and attracted the students' attention. That passage was titled '[7]Oliver Twist Asks for More'. Once the teacher began explaining, the boys became so excited and exclaimed out loud at the events in the story. As the story goes, Oliver, who was an orphan, was admitted into an orphanage. In this shelter, the boys were offered a small amount of food, which instead of satisfying their hunger, kept them in a state of permanent starvation. One day, as they finished eating their ration, at a particular table, one big boy threatened to eat the boy sleeping next to him if he did not get more.

Hearing all that, the boys in my class got so excited; they pounded their desks, yelled at each, "Hey! Did you hear that? Did you hear that?" And the

---

[7] Oliver Twist, a famous novel from the English literature, was written by the well-known author Charles Dickens in 1837-1839.

teacher had a hard time keeping discipline that day. He did not understand the reason for this sudden excitement among those boys who were normally half asleep while he was explaining the other texts.

The events in Oliver's story, as they unfolded, became more thrilling. After hearing the threat from that big boy, the children in that orphanage held a council and the decision fell on to Oliver Twist to walk to the master after serving dinner and ask for more. Oliver was afraid to resist and accepted the council decision. That night after the food was served and eaten by the boys in a moment, they whispered to each other and winked at Oliver and his neighbours pushed him to act. Oliver, under that pressure, carried his plate and walked to the master and said, "Please, sir, I want some more." The master was shocked, silence fell, and the hall was filled with tension. The boys, aware of the crime just being committed, trembled with fear. How dare this little rebel ask for more? That was unprecedented. When the amazed master asked Oliver in a faint voice to repeat, Oliver innocently repeated his request.

The master aimed a blow at Oliver's head with his ladle, pulled his hair and rushed him into the board's room. He cried, "Oliver Twist asks for more." The board members were shocked. One said that this boy should be hanged. The next day, an ad was pasted on the gate offering five pounds to any man or woman who would take Oliver as an apprentice in any trade or business. In other words, because Oliver asked for more food, he was sold into slavery.

The students, who usually daydreamed during the other lessons, were so excited by Oliver's story that they paid very good attention. During the session, they shouted support for Oliver and cursed the master, the board members and anyone that participated in Oliver's trial. *They even wanted to start a solidarity movement to support Oliver*. They took notes and wrote meanings. They asked the teacher if this was a real story. In the canteen whenever a fight erupted with the cooks, the boys shouted, "Oliver asks for more." But this time, it was not the British Oliver, it was the Jordanian Oliver. Indeed, the boys had been so engaged in the session that they participated and enjoyed every minute. So, Oliver Twist became extremely popular at school and the boys almost erected a monument for him. The English teacher once said that he wished that the whole book would be like Oliver's story, but sadly it was not.

In hindsight, we were overjoyed at the story of Oliver Twist because we identified with Oliver, and he became our hero for challenging the authorities and asking for more. Both our boarding school and Oliver's orphanage had tough rules and harsh staff. The similarity between Oliver's and the other orphans' suffering and ours made us live in the story and aroused our curiosity to know every detail. It is concluded that language learners, wherever they are, will be highly motivated and will interact very actively with the material if they have some background knowledge of the situation.

If, for example, Oliver woke up every morning, ate cornflakes, kissed his mom goodbye, got on the bus to school, the students would have felt bored as usual, and would not have been able to comprehend because they had a completely different lifestyle at the boarding school or when they joined their folk in the desert. However, they enjoyed the story about Oliver because life at school was somehow like Oliver's orphanage.

Our class, Second Secondary, one year before graduation, was nicknamed Oliver Twist's orphanage. And many students from the other classes expected us to be kicked out of school or displayed for sale one by one. It was true that in that section, we became so obsessed with Oliver's story that we retold it time after time to other students and friends from other sections.

One day, we had a weird idea; I and some classmates decided to enact Oliver's story in the canteen. So, we met and distributed the roles. We, cleverly, gave Oliver's role to one boy who was bad tempered and a Bedouin in the sense that he would fight for his dignity and would not accept insults. Even his name (Zaal), by coincidence, meant anger. So, we anticipated an exciting scene in the canteen. I took the role of the boy who threatens to eat someone. Then we rehearsed twice in the barracks and got ready for the play.

The following day, at lunch, our group consisted of five students, and we sat around one table. As all of us were licking our plates and still feeling hungry, I cleared my throat and spoke in a deep low voice looking angrily at the other boys on the table, "I am still starving, and I am going to eat the boy sleeping next to me tonight if I do not get more." I threatened. Hearing that, the boys got frightened and all looked at Zaal, the boy supposed to be Oliver and hissed, "Go Oliver. Go, ask for more. This boy will eat someone. Go." Zaal, the Oliver of Jordan hesitated a little, but everyone was urging him to go. So, he stood up, took a deep breath, and walked steadily to the service booth. We were giggling and elbowing each other waiting for the exciting scene.

The Oliver Twist of Jordan stood there at the booth looking at the cooks stretching his empty plate toward them.

"What do you want?" asked the fat cook.

"I want some more food. I am still hungry," Oliver said.

"We have given you your ration and we are still serving other boys. Can't you see the line?"

"But I am hungry, and I want more," Oliver insisted.

"Go away now and come back later. We will give you some if there is any left."

"No. I want some now."

"Shut up and go way. You are obstructing the line. No more food," the cook yelled.

"You shut up. Have more respect," Oliver roared.

"Call the teacher on duty," shouted the cook.

As the Oliver of Jordan could hear the boys laughing and banging their mess hall kits, and some were shouting 'fight Zaal fight', he lost his temper, and to avenge his hurt pride, he tossed his plate at the cook who retaliated by throwing his big ladle at him. The teacher on duty, a lieutenant, dashed inside, silence fell, and the teacher hit Zaal with his stick very hard and dragged him into detention. Our Oliver spent one day in detention and was given one warning. He was told that if he repeated this, he would be expelled.

Although we had a great time watching the Oliver Twist of Jordan's episode in the mess hall, we felt guilty about that Bedouin boy because we pushed him into that nightmare. And when he was released from detention, we gave him a hero's welcome and thanked God he was not sold into slavery. The story spread in the school, and it became a fun topic for staff and students. Zaal said, "I will never be Oliver anymore. Even if you pay me money." We burst out laughing. One teacher was heard saying, "If these students have all this energy, creativity, and imagination, why don't we start a theatre group here in this military school? This would be the first of its kind in Jordan."

When I was qualifying as an English teacher many years later, I had kept Oliver's image in my mind and the first book I promised myself to read, after advancing my English of course, was the full story of Oliver as I wanted to know what happened to him later. In fact, Charles Dickens' books filled a lot of my time at university until the early hours in the morning. However, the main problem was that with each page, I had to stop frequently to search the dictionary for meanings rather than reading. Sometimes, the English Arabic dictionary did not offer the right synonym and the whole meaning stayed vague. I wondered why Charles Dickens and Shakespeare before him wrote in such incomprehensible language. "Do native speakers understand all this? Don't they need the dictionary?" I asked myself. I envied them and I wished I had been born British or Canadian so I could enjoy reading without the hateful frequent interruption of dictionary checking. Although I hated the dictionary sometimes, I admitted the dictionary was my best friend and my saviour.

As a last resort, I had to refer to the English-English Dictionary, which led me into more problems as the word's explanation contained words that I did not know, and I was in doubt! This reminded me of the Arabic adage, 'the water is interpreted as water'. Thus, another round of searching for meanings took place. That was time consuming. I had to live that dilemma tens of times every day that took hours and hours. Sometimes, I thrust the dictionary on the table and cursed the day I decided to be an English teacher. The stack of all kinds of dictionaries on my desk, from Cambridge, to Webster, to Oxford, etc., reminded the observer what kind of a student I was. I used to save money from my small allowance just to buy dictionaries.

When I reflect on the Oliver Twist of Jordan's episode in my journey to learn English, I feel nostalgic as I miss everyone that participated in that part of my life, like classmates, friends, teachers and even the cooks who enjoyed seeing us starving. And I excuse the cooks for being mean to us because if they had been generous and given us more than the ration, many students would have ended up without food and they would have been held responsible by the school seniors. Oliver Twist of England made me love English literature and renewed my confidence that this literature is rich and can be understood and expelled the belief from my mind that it is too hard and complex.

Chapter 5
"Study English Because You Have the Right Aptitude"

It is now the year 1970 and I am 20 years old. I do not know how I passed the public exam and managed to obtain a school leaving certificate, the General certificate of Secondary Education (GCSE). This to ordinary people in our culture is the greatest achievement in a person's life and the door that opens a new life for a rising young man or a young woman. After 12 years of attending boring classes and being manipulated by merciless teachers, and memorising whole books, from cover to cover, finally you pass the public exam. Now you are crowned holder of the Baccalaureate General as was known by people in the 1970s.

I compare the earning of the Baccalaureate General to the acquisition of Ali Baba's secret word *'Open Sesame'*. Have you heard of Ali Baba? Ali Baba, according to the tale 'Ali Baba and the 40 Thieves,' in the One Thousand and One Nights famous Arabic tales, managed to steal the thieves' secret word, *'Open Sesame',* that opened the cave where they had stored their stolen treasures. This possession of 'Open Sesame' transformed Ali Baba from a very poor wood cutter into a very rich man. However, the main difference is that Ali Baba did not do any hard work to obtain that secret.

By holding the Baccalaureate General, a person holds the key to higher education anywhere in the world. However, the real 'Open Sesame' is the lavish generosity of families and siblings and friends of the one who had just passed the GCSE exam. He or she is given gifts, congratulations are published in the newspapers, and celebration like singing, dancing, and distributing sweets continued for some days.

In addition to being a great family event, it is also a national event as people celebrate in the streets and public places through days and nights. However, there is one problem, some excited family members, or friends fire shots from their guns in the air to express their happiness which tragically kills some people sometimes and celebrations turn into mourning.

The GCSE is the 'Open Sesame' to your family's money, love, sympathy, and almost all your wishes are granted. It is also the 'Open Sesame' to join university, besides, if your family is well off enough, you have a chance of studying abroad. I live in a culture that values education and community members place education at the top of their priorities. If a school leaving certificate opens the hearts and minds of all people around you, it is also the 'Open Sesame' to a university degree, which is considered the highest achievement of a community member. Equally important, people believe that a university degree is the 'Open Sesame' to the infinite treasure of the world, a stable job.

Now forget all that I have said about the GCSE and the 'Open Sesame' because it is not applicable to me. I was the odd man out according to all cultural values and beliefs. Being an orphan, lonely in this world, and with older brothers who turned their backs on me and did not feel any commitment as brothers to my misfortune, my well-earned Baccalaureate General, the dream of every schoolboy or girl and their 'Open Sesame' to happiness, backfired and my 'Open Sesame' opened a world of anxiety, uncertainty, and loss. I had no idea what to do in my life. I tried to join the military, but I failed the vision test. That perhaps was a good omen, and I thanked my God for failing the vision test.

I travelled to Damascus to meet my two brothers who had moved there. For some time, I stayed with my second oldest brother and frequented some old school friends who had been studying at Damascus University. As I listened to their talk about their daily life, I envied them and dreamt of joining Damascus University or any university. I just dreamed of being like any human being. I knew that was just one of a million wishes but 'beggars cannot be choosers.'

I was getting worried as we were entering September and I had not been enlisted in anything. All my friends and classmates from my batch had found a direction and they were following their dreams. The only institution that had welcomed me was the streets of Damascus. There I could pace, loiter, and look at shop windows free of charge.

One evening in September as I was sitting with some friends in Damascus, my two brothers emerged from nowhere and told me that they would be dropping me at Damascus Airport to catch a flight to Algeria. When I tried to open my mouth, they signalled to me to hurry so I do not miss the plane and end up pacing Damascus' streets. On the way to the airport, I tried to get some answers about why I was going to Algeria, and all I heard from the two brothers was that I was going to study. What exactly I was going to study was none of their business. While I was sitting in the back seat of that old Land Cruiser, empty handed with neither luggage nor money, I felt like a convict being transported to jail.

All the information about Algeria that I had possessed came from the geography lessons at school. However, most of that information had evaporated after taking the geography exam. All I knew is it is a mountainous country and is very vast. Nevertheless, Algeria had a special place in my memory because when I was at primary school in the late 1950s, we used to chant the Algerian Revolution National Anthem in every morning assembly before going into classes. All I knew at that time was that the Algerians, who are Arabs and Muslims, had been engaged in a bloody war to rid themselves of the French colonisers. We were told that it was our duty to support them, and I remember donating my little allowance to the revolution sometimes. It had never crossed my mind that I would be going to that Northern African Country to build my future.

The most popular Algerian revolutionary figure that everyone remembered was Jamila Buhairid whose personality was woven into a fairy tale in most Arab countries. Her struggle against the French, her imprisonment, torture at the hands of the colonisers was on every tongue. Jamila entered history when she, one day at school, refused to repeat the slogan, 'France is our mother', and instead she stood up and shouted, "Algeria is our mother."

Arriving at Damascus Airport, my brothers introduced me to someone who was my age but looked confident and self-assured, in contrast, I felt bewildered, uncertain, and unsure. There, I discovered that I was going to be part of a group of Palestinian students who had been given scholarships to study in Algeria, at the invitation of the Algerian government. Algeria had a special relationship with the Palestine Liberation Organisation (PLO), and it took the burden of hosting many Palestinian students.

In a while, I found myself shaking hands with some young Palestinians that I had never met before. I could hear people talking in a distinctive Palestinian accent which I could recognise even though among millions of other Arabs. In a short time, I would be flying to Algeria with more than a hundred Palestinian students that had converged at Damascus Airport from their countries of diaspora. Now, having the feeling that I was not the only one heading toward an unknown destiny, I began to get back some of self-confidence and my anxiety began to ease.

Putting my hand in my pocket, I felt a piece of paper which turned out to be a 20 American dollar note that was handed to me by my eldest brother before turning his back on me. This would be the first time I had seen the green backs; besides, it would be the biggest amount of money I had ever put in my pocket. In contrast, I discovered later that this amount would be, perhaps, sufficient for one day's expenditure in Algiers.

As I stood facing my two brothers, one of them looked me straight in the face and uttered his words slowly and emphatically, "This is your last and only chance to rise in the world. The Algerian government will take full care of you. Study hard, get a degree then a job. Algeria is the land of opportunity for you. Do not come back." They kissed me goodbye and hurried out. As I watched them rushing out, they looked like a couple who have just abandoned something illegal.

Being young and being only 20 years old and still living under the foolish illusion that my brothers will stand up for their duties toward their brother, an orphan, I did not take their words, 'do not come back', seriously and I went back a year later. That return was one of the worst episodes of my young life.

As we stood on the Tarmac to board the airplane, I felt so excited at the sight of the aircraft and how majestic it looked. This would be my first time to board an aircraft. Suddenly, those young Palestinians rushed to the plane stairway, and they started pushing, jostling, elbowing each other to get into the aircraft first. Then some more rammed from the back into the crowd and those in the middle got squeezed. It looked like a stampede.

I stood astonished and thanked my military upbringing at the military boarding school that had taught me self-discipline and respect for the queue. At the military boarding school, if you jumped the queue at lunch, you would be caned, deprived of lunch, and might be sent into detention. That kind of training, although very harsh, made us one of the most disciplined children in the world.

"Who are those people?" An elderly passenger standing next to me watching the stampede asked drily in a Syrian accent.

"I do not know," I said turning my lips up and shaking my head.

This encouraged him to make a strong comment. "They are acting like '*hamad*g,' Arabic for 'savages coming from jungles.'" I kept my mouth shut and ignored his comments. I felt so proud of myself that I was not taking part in that *'hamadg'* action.

During the flight, the crew had a hard time trying to control those young people who kept talking so loudly to each other. Of course, they disturbed other passengers. To my shock, they even wanted to dance *dabk*a, Palestinian folkloric dance in the aircraft aisle while we were flying at almost 43, 000 feet high. I read some verses from the Holy Quran.

Suddenly, the plane plunged down for a few seconds and the 'fasten your seat belts' sign was illuminated. Another little plunge and a voice in English and Arabic came on the intercom telling us that we were entering an area of turbulence and we had to stay seated and keep our seat belts fastened. I felt so scared.

"What is that? What is turbulence?" I wondered loudly.

"They are holes in space like holes in the ground," someone next to me said.

"You mean we are flying on an unpaved road." All gave a nervous laugh.

Another whispered, "This is Syrian Air. You know. This plane is just like their old buses and taxis that had served in WW2."

To my disbelief, the plane was jumping and dancing worse than our village bus when it fell in ditches and holes on our village unpaved roads. As children, we had a lot of fun sitting on the back seat on the bus bouncing like a ball. Since it was my first air trip, I felt so scared in this aircraft which looked like a sardine can. This was a slow death. Now everybody was quiet, but you could hear funeral prayers. Those who wanted to dance sank in their seats and looked nervous. Nobody wanted to dance now, let the aircraft dance.

When we arrived at Algiers Airport, a surprise was waiting for me. When the check in officer asked me for my vaccination health card, I had no idea what he meant by that. I got more confused because I could not understand the Algerian officer's accent which sounded strange. The Palestinian standing behind me showed me his health card, so I understood. Then, I was instructed to stand aside and wait because I was obstructing the long queue of passengers. While waiting, I felt like someone with a contagious disease that had to be quarantined. Later, I felt very relieved when another Palestinian joined me. We looked at each other, laughed and shook hands. That was the beginning of a friendship.

Later, an official came and told us that we would be taken to the health detention centre at the airport where we would stay a few days before we are allowed into the country. I and my friend began to speculate about the so-called detention. We feared that it could be another word for jail or prison. What kind of treatment would we receive? I was young and had little experience in life. However, all these questions would be answered later.

We followed an official from the airport to a room where we met a couple who looked like Europeans, of course, the four of us were guilty of not carrying a vaccination card. That was our crime. Now we were nervous about the punishment and how severe it would be. We looked at each other, smiled, shook hands and we shared one destiny. Later, the four of us, the only passengers at Algiers Airport that had no health cards, were driven to a far way building by a very friendly official.

We noticed with amusement that we had considerable difficulty in communicating with Algerians. We realised that their Arabic was so different from ours. We noticed they were mixing Arabic with words from French, as we guessed. We saw that they spoke to each other in French and in a strange form of Arabic with us. Although it was hard to understand, we managed to get the message through. However, the language issue became a serious barrier for deeper understanding in the coming days.

The quarantine centre, which was small, to our delight, turned to be a kind of a five-star guest house. We were offered comfortable accommodation, delicious food, and very nice treatment. We were the only supposed to be patients in that centre and enjoyed receiving all the attention. For two days, we ate, talked, and slept very well. We even joked with the friendly staff that there was no pressure to release us, and they could keep us as long as they wanted. "Are you sure we are free of any contagious diseases?" we joked.

The detention period at Algiers Airport was a very important chapter in my story with the English language. The presence of the young Canadian couple was the first test of my English ability. They were friendly, talkative, and curious about the Palestinian question. I was very disappointed with myself as I remember I could express no more than 50% or less of what I wanted to say. Let alone my produced speech was a very corrupted form of English. Accuracy was disastrous; I had made mistakes in all aspects such as grammar, pronunciation, and tenses mixing up *do, did, does, have, has, had and so on*. However, the most frustrating part of the conversation was finding the right word. I think that my wealth of vocabulary those days did not exceed 500 words.

To get my message across to those people, I depended a lot on my nonverbal language. I discovered how powerful body language can be. In fact, I had some experience in sign language as in the village I had an uncle who was speech impaired. My father managed to communicate with him, and he taught me some sign language. I felt so happy when he understood my message.

If I wanted to assess my spoken English at that time by the current International English Testing System (IELTS) standards, I would give my ability at that time no more than band 3, or 3.5. My spoken English would be described as follows: [8]"*He cannot respond without noticeable pauses, frequent repetition and self-correction, some breakdowns in coherence, produces basic sentence forms and some correct simple sentences but subordinate structures are rare, errors are frequent and may lead to misunderstanding, mispronunciations are frequent and cause some difficulty for the listener, able to talk about familiar topics to some extent.* **Can put strain on the listener**." 'Putting pressure on the listener, in my opinion as an English teacher, is the biggest barrier to communicate with others.

In spite of putting strain on the Canadians, they showed tolerance and sympathy, and they kept saying, "Go…go, you are doing well. We understand." This attitude encouraged me, and I was not hindered by language anxiety. Besides, my Palestinian friend was even poorer than me and we both struggled to explain our emotions about the Palestinian people's disaster. The Palestinian issue has been my highest priority in any situation, and I would take advantage of any opportunity to present our people's problem to the world.

From an early age, I learned that quiet diplomacy can be the most effective weapon in the world. My educated father had raised me to believe that *the pen is mightier than the sword, and the word is mightier than the gun.*

The Canadian couple were very receptive and understanding of the Palestinian tragedy. They had been so keen to get some insight into the Arab Israeli conflict. Their previous knowledge came from Israeli Zionist propaganda. The Arabs in the 70s did not need any publicity or propaganda because by carrying out a series of high jacking of international flights and destroying passengers' planes in the middle of the day in the Jordanian desert with international media transmitting those horrible acts live to the world, the Arabs and the Palestinians presented themselves to the world as terrorists. As a result, most people in America, in the West, and in many parts of the world became convinced that Palestinians were a bunch of terrorists, and the Israelis were innocent victims. Thus, changing people's perception became very challenging.

---

[8] Information has been taken from IELTS speaking band descriptors.

The situation in the Middle East was so complex. With my poor English and insufficient knowledge of history and world affairs, I could not explain the story properly to the Canadians. That would be my first ever encounter with people from the West.

After two days, we packed and left the detention centre. We said goodbye to the nice Canadian couple, and we promised to write to each other, but I do not remember if we did because my English was not good enough to write an understandable letter.

I remember while we were staying in the quarantine centre at Algiers Airport, the Canadian lady once said something that was engraved in my memory.

She said, "Ghassoub. I think you should study English because you have the right ap…tit…u…" She said something I did not understand.

"Sorry. What you means {sic} by ap…ap…*what is meaning* {sic} *that word you saying* {sic}." I asked hesitantly in my corrupt English.

She spelled the word slowly. "I mean *a p t i t u d e*, aptitude, aptitude," she explained.

"Aptitude, aptitude," I repeated after her. *Wow, that is a big word*, I thought. "It means you like languages, and you have a natural desire to learn. You also pick up quickly. Besides, you want to know. You see you are asking about meanings."

Her husband and my Palestinian companion, who were listening, nodded their heads in agreement.

Until that moment, three important people had encouraged me to study English. Charlotte of the Dead Sea, when I was around 9:00, Mr. Waleed my primary school teacher, and now this Canadian lady. I was 20 years old at that time. I felt so motivated to study English, but I had no idea if English was taught in Algeria. I had zero knowledge of Algeria's higher education system. How could my brothers send me into the unknown? I knew they just wanted me to get off their backs. "Don't come back." That was the last thing they said to me.

In retrospect, this was appropriate career advice given in good faith. I became determined to do just that. I thought to myself, *the most thing she praised, which qualified me to be a strong candidate to study English, was my courage to talk despite the endless mistakes. That is the right aptitude she emphasised.*

This enhanced my knowledge of the word 'aptitude.' That was hilarious. Aptitude became my buzz word for a while. And whenever the other Palestinian boys, some of whom would become very close friends, asked me why I wanted to study English, I would reply pretending to be very confident, "Because I have the right aptitude."

"What is that?" they asked.

I felt so proud of knowing a word that no one else knew.

This accidental encounter with that Canadian couple proved decisive in my life and happened at the right moment. A year after that encounter, while almost every Palestinian student was at a loss and could not decide on a major to study because they had never been advised on what to major in, I walked into the English Department at Oran university and registered as a new student without any hesitation. That was the beginning of my story with the English language.

After doing all check in formalities at Algiers Airport, we bid final goodbye to the Canadians and stood outside the airport waiting for someone from the Palestinian embassy, or I should say 'bureau,' to give us a left to join the group. Suddenly, my Palestinian companion shook my shoulder with an inquisitive look in his eyes pointing to his suitcase saying in alarm.

"Hey, man. You are going to delay us more because I do not see your luggage, where is your suitcase? Oh my God you must have forgotten it. Do not tell me we are going back to the airport authorities."

I put my hand on his shoulder and said indifferently. "Do not worry. I do not have any luggage," I continued while the shock did not leave his face.

"Well. Do you remember that I borrowed your shaver and even this sweater I am wearing that you lent me to protect me from the cold? You never asked about my luggage."

I told him the story of my brothers descending on me out of the blue and dragging me to Damascus Airport.

"There was no time to go back to my brother's house and collect my suitcase. In fact, it is not a real suitcase; it is made of cardboard with metal cap on the corners. It is not like yours. Besides, I had very few clothes to worry about. Luckily, I had to leave it because I would be ashamed carrying it now."

"You mean you did not know that you were going on a scholarship to Algeria?" he asked.

"Not at all. They simply snapped that I was going on a scholarship to study in Algeria that night. What about you? Did you know earlier?"

"Oh yes. I had known weeks before," he said.

I continued, "My brothers dropped me at the airport, gave me some money and left. They said I would buy clothes and other necessities in Algeria."

"So, they must have given you a lot of money," he said excitedly.

I hesitated and looked ahead without speaking.

"Ah! It must be a big amount and you do not want to reveal the secret," he remarked.

"20 $," I said indifferently.

That was jaw-dropping. The shock on my newly acquired friend was indescribable.

"What? That is incredible. You are going abroad with no suitcase, and only 20$. This would not buy you a shirt here in Algeria. I do not know! That is crazy. If I were you, I would have protested and asked for more."

"My oldest brother is an officer, too authoritarian, and I would not dare asking him for anything. Besides, he would not listen."

My friend, who looked more mature than his age, said as the shock had not left his face, "Sorry to hear that. This is really the most unusual story I have heard so far." Then he added while shaking his head in disbelief. "How can a young man be sent abroad with ONLY 20$ and nothing else?"

"Everything is possible in my brothers' philosophy. They see the world as black and white…No leeway!"

"Look. I have 300 dollars and I could lend you some if the authorities delayed our scholarship. I think we will have a monthly allowance from the government. Besides, I can ask for more from my family."

"300$," I exclaimed. "That is wealth. You are a millionaire." We both laughed and did a high five.

When we joined the rest of the group, to my disbelief, the students had been accommodated in a massive military barracks that had belonged to the French army during the colonial period. The barracks was as big as three or four barracks where I had spent my boyhood in at the boarding military school in Jordan. I felt dismayed at my misfortune and wondered if I was going to spend my whole life in military barracks.

My thoughts were interrupted by the embassy's representative who assured us that this was a temporary lodging until the authorities could find us decent places to stay at. He explained that Algeria and the capital in particular suffers from one of the most severe accommodation crises in the world. There is nothing to rent, and if a unit is available, it is too expensive, besides, people are suspicious and hesitate to rent to anyone. Finally, he looked at us and said, "This is a different place."

Indeed, it was.

After two weeks of living in that barracks suffering from the rotten blankets and shivering from October cold at night, the authorities accommodated us in small hotels and furnished accommodations scattered all over the city that belonged to the socialist government.

Algeria, under [9]Boumediene adopted a socialist system in running the economy. In the 70s under that system, individual ownership was extremely limited as the government owned almost everything. The country felt like a big residential compound run by one management. However, the system was too complex to understand. Whether it was socialism or capitalism, Algerians treated us very kindly. They gave us free accommodation, a monthly allowance, and free education. They did all this under the slogan, 'help a brother in need.' They treated us like Algerians. Algeria was a refuge for many young people from third world countries who had been offered free education and opportunities to work. What was amazing was that Algeria wanted nothing from us in return. Algeria in the 70s looked like [10]*Plato's Republic*. They helped foreigners without regard to their ethnic or political views.

I had never thought that my little allowance that I had donated to the Algerian Revolution when I was a child in the 1950s would be such an investment in my future in the 1970s. That was an incredible return for some piasters and some coins; the Algerian government had undertaken to sponsor my higher education from A to Z without my committing myself to any preconditions. Algeria was my home for seven years.

---

[9] Boumediene: Algerian President from 1965 until his death in 1978.

[10] Plato, the Geek philosopher, in 375 BC created a dialogue about justice, the order and character of the just city-state, and the just man.

Chapter 6
Be a Doctor or an Engineer or Disappear

It's 1979. Now we Palestinian students are residents of Algiers, one of the most crowded cities in the world. Algiers in those days looked like a European city in most areas. We felt privileged to have been given the chance to live there. After having settled in a room with other four students, the discussion began about our future. Our fate was in the hands of the Palestinian embassy. We had many questions we hoped would be answered in our first meeting with the Revolution's Representative, Abu Jalil, who was given the rank of ambassador by the Algerian government. It was obvious that the Algerian government treated the PLO's official as first-class diplomats.

The meeting took place in the embassy's basement which was turned into a big meeting hall. We were nudging each other that this hall, according to rumours, was a dungeon where Algerian detainees had been tortured by the brutal colonial French police. Some of those detainees died under torture. We exchanged looks as if saying that this hall might resume its past but by a different authority. So, we cautioned each other that in the coming meeting, "Watch your mouth and make sure you do not challenge the authority a lot." Abu Jalil can deport you on the spot.

In the middle of all that negative pessimistic thinking arrived the ambassador, Abu Jalil. He was notorious for being very sectarian, tough minded, unapproachable, very authoritarian, and very sharp and sarcastic. He looked stylish in his business suit, and we wondered whether he represented a revolution or an oil producing country.

Abu Jalil started by reminding us that we represented the Palestinian people and we had to behave properly in public and in private. He claimed that he held the authority to get anyone deported for violation of good conduct. He gave a list of the seven sins which included women, alcohol and so on. Those were abundantly available for anyone willing to commit sins. That did not worry me because I had my priorities. Then he outlined his policy and the Palestinian leadership's vision concerning our education.

In an a dictatorial tone that was not open to negotiation, he said, "Abu Ammar," referring to Yasser Arafat (Head of the Revolutionary Council) by his nom de guerre, "wants every Palestinian in higher education to become either a doctor or an engineer. This is how you can serve your revolution and your country."

I nodded my head in agreement, but I whispered, "Not everyone has the *aptitude* to be this or that. Abu Jalil has no idea of educational psychology."

He declared, "This year is a preparation year and everyone without exception has to study French as it is the language of instruction at higher education in Algerian institutions. The leadership needs cadres that build the country."

"Which country is he talking about?" I asked myself. "All Palestine is under Israeli occupation. Ah! I think he meant after liberation!" I looked up into the ceiling and murmured, "God! Please give me a second life to see that day."

A murmur went through the audience, and one could see many had raised their hands to ask questions. The ambassador, who was very sarcastic, did not mind questions but almost all his replies were negative. "I want to study something I like, something I am passionate about," one boy said. Another said that to be a doctor, or an engineer was his mother's dream, but he is from the Arts stream and he is so poor in mathematics. Another complained that he would fail and waste years on something he would not be able do. The ambassador shunned all that by saying that was his final offer; take it or leave it.

He emphasised that we had to challenge ourselves and study something valuable. All protests fell on deaf ears and the ambassador, who owned the power of deporting any agitator, stuck to his guns. Although I felt excited about studying French, I hated the idea of immersing myself in medicine or engineering. I did not even know the multiplication table properly. I love poetry contests, literary prose, debates, but cutting up human bodies or dissecting body organs is not my game.

As there was no chance of resisting, we resigned ourselves to Abu Jalil's plans. Without any delay, the embassy contracted the Alliance Francaise, the best and the only French institute in Algiers, to organise French courses for us. So, from October 1970 to June 1971, we did nothing but just attending French lessons on a daily basis. The teacher, who was a native speaker, employed the state-of-the-art methods and technology by that era's standards. He taught through French as, luckily, he did not know Arabic, he used a projector, a tape recorder, flash cards, illustrations, acting, and group work. That was really fascinating as we had never seen such methodology. We had learnt English at school through grammar translation methods which gave us a few words, and some grammar rules. *If I had been taught English at school for nine years through our French teacher's methods, I would challenge Shakespeare now,* I thought.

By the end of the course in June, I and those who took it seriously and attended classes regularly, achieved a kind of intermediate level in French. In retrospect, I thanked the ambassador for forcing us to learn French because in later years my French skill would bring about a major breakthrough in my life. I almost became a French citizen. Learning French was like a visa to enter and live in France, one of the most beautiful countries in the world.

That was the end of our first academic year in Algeria. Within those five or six months, I had learnt French and could make conversation on familiar topics and write simple short letters. I considered that my greatest achievement at that time. I concluded that in less than six months, I had learned more French than I had learned English in nine years at school.

We were told to go home for the summer and come back in August to join university. The authorities explained that they needed our accommodation for the many delegations that would be visiting Algiers that summer. Algiers on those days hosted conferences, seminars, symposiums for liberation and independence movements from Africa, Latin America, and Asia. It was a haven for revolutionaries from all over the world. It was a hive of activities. For example, one of the common sights was posters carrying the pictures and sayings of Che Guevara, the international revolutionary figure until the late 1960s.

Another example, '*Guantanamera*' maybe the best-known Cuban song and that country's most celebrated patriotic one, became one of our favourite revolutionary songs.

I did not have a home to go to; my country was under occupation, my parents were dead, and my brothers' hearts and homes were locked as well. As we had to vacate our rooms, I had no choice but to travel back to Syria where my brothers lived. After returning to Damascus in the summer of 1971, I fell into such bitter conflicts with my two brothers and their wives that I had to spend most of my time at my second youngest brother's tiny home in the Damascus refugee camp.

I knew that I had committed a mistake by returning and I should have stayed in Algiers at any cost. I vowed not to go back to Damascus again and end this torture. But I did not keep that vow either. Reflecting on this now, until that moment, I had not developed the ability to act more independently. This was due to the fact my mother used to do everything for me before she died.

Chapter 7
My Writing Struggle and the 'I' Grade

At the Palestinian Embassy in Algiers, the only place where we Palestinian students found refuge, we received some news, both good and bad news: we were told that the ambassador had modified his weighty demand on us to study engineering and medicine, instead he advised us to study these majors. That was an implicit message that we were free to study the subject we preferred. I rejoiced and felt happy for the first time in months. However, we had some shocking news: many of the students in our cohort, including me, had been transferred to Oran, Algeria's second largest city located around 400 kms from the capital. The embassy justified this decision by claiming that it was impossible to accommodate us at the university dorms in Algiers while Oran had plenty of free accommodation.

Many accused the embassy of racial discrimination as those students banished to Oran belonged to another breed, not the ambassador's breed. Some boys rebelled, raised their voices in the embassy and there was a small riot. "We know that you have accommodated your relatives and friends, it is obvious," some voices in the back shouted. I kept my mouth shut because if I got deported, there would be no place to go to.

You must understand it well that Algeria is the only refuge for you in this world, I warned myself. *So do not behave badly.*

Staff dismissed all that and our transfer was effective from that moment. "Go to Oran or you will be deported." I did not take part in that mini riot, and I was one of the wise voices that had urged those rebels to call it off. I was the first one to board the bus to Oran. I wondered from where that wisdom, patience, and insight came to me at that time. I thought I had inherited those traits from my father. But my life since my mother's death and my country's occupation had taught me how to survive in this merciless world.

I loved Oran at first sight. It was less crowded, cosy, and the atmosphere was intimate as opposed to Algiers where you feel like an alien. What I loved most was Oran's Sea front; it was breath-taking, and I used to spend hours walking or sitting on café terraces there. The boulevard along the seashore provided an incredibly beautiful view of the surrounding cliffs and the old Santa Cruz church. Algerians still used the French name of that boulevard: Front de Mer.

Finally, I began to follow my dream and I joined (*la Faculté des Lettres, section d'Anglais*) Faculty of Arts, the English section. I was then a proud member of the English Department. This department had been set up some years before by a very dynamic Algerian academic who after interviewing me in English, was not very impressed but he encouraged me to try and advised me that I had to work very hard to catch up with other students.

I felt worried but I was determined to follow my English dream. I knew that my admission into the English Department was done to increase the number of students in that new department. What a joke but that was the truth. If I had been given an entry test, I would have never been admitted into the English section. Luckily, admission rules at Oran University were not tough and that was my greatest luck. Beginner's luck. [11]"It is almost sure that when you play cards, the first time you are almost sure to win." Indeed, I was playing the English card for the first time in my life.

When I joined the English section as a freshman, I was the only Palestinian and I felt very alienated as Algerian students chatted in French among themselves and communicated with me in their Arabic which was difficult to understand. To my disappointment, my French at that time enabled me to have a limited conversation and I felt very lonely, as well as having poor English. I spent most of my time either in the library or standing in the corridor and chatting with passing by Palestinians.

As I started attending lectures and seminars, I began to discover how poor my English was. The teaching staff consisted mostly of native speakers of English, a few Algerians and one or two from other Arab countries. The department was so small that everyone knew everyone. As I sat listening to lectures, I was haunted by some ghost: one was the teachers' accents, the second was vocabulary because those lecturers were using big words that were beyond my 500-1000 words. Thirdly, they talked so fast that I could not take any notes.

---

[11] 'Taken from The Alchemist by Paulo Coelho.

We did not have any textbooks and instructors taught anything they considered relevant, sometimes giving handouts. In the end, I sat slouching in my chair, my pen rested lifeless on an empty page of my notebook, my perception was blocked, and my whole system was not functioning. I just did not know what to do. I felt myself a stranger in a strange land.

While I was at least a sleeping student in the English Department, a big number of Palestinian students were hopping from one department to another like grasshoppers, as they were trying to settle in a major. In the beginning, the majority joined the medicine faculty hoping to be doctors one day. This hope faded very quickly, and those students faced the reality that they might spend their whole life in the medicine major and might not earn it.

One of those students decided to hang on to that false hope and it is said that he kept repeating for twenty years. What helped him survive was that the Algerian higher education authorities did not force any student to withdraw because of failure and one could repeat as many times as he or she wanted. This particular student persisted and became a legend.

At Oran University, lecture rooms were open to the public, like cinemas, besides, attendance was not compulsory, so you could attend any lecture in any department, and no one would question you. Some Palestinian students, who were running away from medicine and engineering, hopped into the English lectures hoping that their English would help them join the English major. They survived 10 to 15 minutes and then rushed out. As I saw them running away, I smiled bitterly and felt more desperate because I was hoping that one of them would stay so I could share my misery with him.

They later told me that they did not understand anything and wondered how I would survive in English and what the hell I was doing there.

"What are you doing there sitting like a deaf person at a wedding party as the proverb goes?" one said.

"Is this English? I did not understand anything," another commented.

"What you heard is real English, but the truth is that your English is not English my poor friend," I shouted. Everyone roared with laughter.

"So, because we do not know modern math, we cannot join medicine. Also, we do not know real English, so we cannot join English. What did they teach us at school for God's Sake?" one wondered.

"They taught you to memorise books and pass the exams," another replied.

Finally, most of the Palestinian students majored in courses that were taught in Arabic like law, Arabic literature, sociology, etc. They were at an advantage because Algeria was in the process of Arabisation. To encourage Algerians to major in Arabic, they simplified the curriculum, and this made it very easy for Palestinians as Arabic is their first language. So, they majored in law, philosophy and so on.

Sitting in lectures and seminars was the most agonising time at that period for me. Just as the Arabic proverbs tells, "Like a deaf, old, haggard man at a wedding party." What doubled my frustration was that my Algerian classmates felt comfortable during the sessions. They seemed to comprehend very well, they also participated well and interacted in English with the teacher and among themselves comfortably. I wondered what made teaching English in North African schools a success while we failed in the Levant. Because of that, I kept my frustration to myself as none of those classmates faced any difficulty. After all, I blamed my schoolteachers and the school system for the misery I was in then.

Although I and the Algerian classmates had just graduated from high school where we spent almost the same number of years, I swore that I would need two more years of intensive English teaching to reach their level or to catch up with them now. I really envied them and ate my heart out when I noticed their self-confidence and the ease with which they managed their learning. It was clear that our school system did not prepare us for higher education and now we were paying the price.

It was really embarrassing to sit among those students because they were light years in their knowledge of English ahead of me. However, the most embarrassing moment was when sometimes I thought I had grasped the information and made a comment and answered a question which turned to be wrong. This triggered some giggling in the seminar and some students looked at me from the corner of their eyes. And you know, when someone turns and look at you from the corner of their eyes, this look conveys hundreds of meanings. I felt their body language was telling me, "Hey, young man from the Levant. You do not belong here. Go and find yourself an Arabic major. Arabic is your native tongue. Why are you wasting your time here?" I felt like an alien.

"But I am not interested in any other major. I love English and it's my dream. What am I going to do with philosophy or geography?"

That is exactly what my Palestinian friends were urging me to do when I discussed my nightmare.

"Come and join the law school. It is so easy and Algerian students beg us for help because their Arabic is poor. Come on, man. At the law department, the situation is the opposite; we are superiors. You will not make it in the English Department. It is too hard. They are not going to open a special slow track for you. Besides, you are the only non-Algerian there." I was as stubborn as a mule and turned a deaf ear to all that.

"I will not give up and will follow my dream whatever the cost might be," I said.

"Then rot there my friend. I am sure that you will come to us after we have already graduated. Good luck! Keep dreaming and one day you may never wake up!" someone mocked.

Although that sounded logical and I was heading nowhere, I refused all advice to change major and decided to continue until I found a way out of this ordeal. I survived by borrowing notes from classmates who happily lent them to me, especially girls. But their French beautiful cursive writing style that I was not used to, made reading notes difficult sometimes and I understood less than 50%. In fact, most students in the department were girls and there were only a few boys, who missed most classes. I didn't know why girls found languages easier!

Then halfway through the semester, came the occasion that revealed my low level of English. One of the courses that we were studying was called written expression. One day, the American teacher gave us a topic and asked us to write an essay at home. I thanked God that it was homework. This would be my first creative writing to be assessed by a native speaker of English. I panicked but I laboured for hours that night to produce the essay. I kept referring to the Arabic English Dictionary, trying to find adequate words. Very often, I would think about the topic in Arabic and translate verbatim into English. I ended up writing one page after a long struggle which I handed to the teacher after convincing myself that I had written a somehow *good* essay.

Then came the shock when the teacher returned our essays with her feedback. As the teacher started distributing the marked essays, I could hear the student shouting with joy as they had received As, Bs, and some Cs. When the teacher handed me my marked essay, I could not believe my eyes, the essay had turned red. I remember writing my essay in blue ink. What had turned it red? Magic! I was transfixed. Literally, the teacher's corrections and comments in red had exceeded my own words in blue. I thought that teacher was practicing embroidery on my paper. If I were that teacher, I would have underlined what was right in that essay to save time. The teacher did not decorate it with the letter F because it was obvious that teacher was sympathetic to my cause, not the Palestinian cause, but being the *odd man out* in that group.

As I looked at that decorated essay, holding my head in my hands like a watermelon, I felt demoralised, and concluded that I would never learn how to write good English. Suddenly, I realised that when you write, it is like confession, you expose yourself and display your mistakes and weaknesses more than in speaking because those mistakes are written, and they attract attention. In other words, you display your scandal in public. My mother used to say, "Do not hang your washing on the neighbours' washing line."

In writing, there is zero tolerance for mistakes and teachers are waiting with their weapon, the red pen. Actually, I became so sensitive to red pens that when I became a teacher of English myself, I very often used green or other colours just to take revenge on that red colour. Red is the colour of blood and I felt that my returned essays in my early semesters at the English Department were dripping with blood.

In my misery, I comforted myself by coming up with my own philosophy. I concluded that, "When you speak, the listener is generally interested in the message, and if your mistake does not impede the meaning, he or she will skip that mistake and you may never discover it. Then it will happen again and again until someone pinpoints it. In an oral dialogue, mistakes are like words *written in the sand* that will be blown by the wind. But in writing, mistakes look like words carved in wood or stone that need a hammer and a chisel to remove them."

The teacher was very sympathetic and understanding. When I met with her later, she said that I had made mistakes in everything: punctuation, spelling, structure, grammar, tenses, and so on. "My advice is not to compare yourself with Algerian students. They have better English because they had better instruction at school. Second, they have a great advantage," she explained.

"What is that?" I asked eagerly. "Their perfect knowledge of French provides a good source of vocabulary and spelling. For example, any noun that ends in 'ion' is pronounced '*syon*' in French, and, '*shen*' in English, but basically has the same spelling and meaning, like the word 'participation.' This doubles their wealth of vocabulary."

"This is fascinating. I did not know that," I said.

Then I began to review my small wealth of words that end in *'tion'*, which would add to my vocabulary account.

She gave me some useful advice on how to improve my writing. However, she cautioned me that it takes time to achieve a good level in writing in a foreign language, and I had to be very patient. "Finally, try your best not to translate from Arabic because English and Arabic have different structures and you need to think in English," she advised.

"Your essay sounded like a poor translation of an Arabic essay," she said.

"How can I think in English? This requires decades of learning. But I will try," I said in a sad voice.

As weeks dragged, I made little improvement and my writing kept changing from black or blue to red. I thought I would never be able to write any accurate understandable English. I once joked with the teacher that I should save her time and write in a red pen. I envied the other students for their good ability in writing. I tried to read, but I found authentic English hard to understand and got bored and gave up because of the overuse of the dictionary. I thought of joining an evening English school, but I was not sure that was available, and if it did, I did not have the money.

Now, I was facing a real dilemma and my motivation to qualify in English began to diminish. I felt, *Now I am in the most critical situation since I arrived in Algeria. The question now is: To be or not to be?*

By the end of the first semester, I received an 'I' which stands for Incomplete in the three English courses that I had joined, namely, oral expression, written expression and grammar. As I had anticipated this, I did not feel the shock. But using an 'I' instead of an 'F' proved to be a very humanitarian gesture because the 'F' tells you, you are a failure, while the 'I' gives you some hope if you try again and the door is still open. In other words, do not give up. Frankly speaking, this had a positive impact on me. I wanted to thank whoever had decided to use the 'I' instead of the 'F'. He/she must have had great knowledge of educational psychology and human nature.

Around five decades later from this encounter with the 'I' versus 'F' concept in grading, one of my students in the college where I was teaching gave a presentation on a very relevant Technology, Entertainment, and Design (TED) talk. That talk was given by Carol Dweck, one of the world's leading researchers in the field of motivation. The talk was titled, *"The power of believing that you can improve."* The secret of the talk is how to avoid 'F' grade [12] with students, which can demoralise them, and instead to use something less harsh.

The presenter quoted Dweck who said, "I heard about a high school in Chicago where students had to pass a certain number of courses to graduate, and if they didn't pass a course, they got the grade *'Not Yet. NY.'"* Neither F nor I.

"And I thought that was fantastic, because if you get a failing grade, you think, I'm nothing, I'm nowhere. But if you get the grade 'Not Yet,' you understand that you're on a learning curve. It gives you a path into the future." (Dweck 2013).

That was exactly the impact on me in my first year in the English Department. The 'I' grade like the 'Not Yet, NY' grade, told me that "You are not a complete failure, and you still stand a chance so do not give up." This is creative, and I urge educators to remove the letter F from their systems. Dweck's talk is a great lesson for all teachers. As educators, we have the power to motivate and demotivate our learners. How often we hear about students or parents who committed suicide because of this damn letter 'F'.

"Seven people commit suicide every day (in India) due to failure in examination."

The 'I' or the 'Not Yet' grade gave me some strength and I kept hanging onto a straw or to a thin twig as the Arabic proverb goes. Failing the three courses was a catastrophe like the loss of my country, Palestine. However, with some encouragement and a little push from sympathetic teachers and friends, I managed to stand up on my feet and continue sailing into rough seas.

The teachers I dealt with had always complimented me heartily on my great attitude and they said that I possessed qualities that qualified me to be a model student regardless of my academic failure. Besides, I was liked and respected by my friends, classmates, and everyone I met. One friend said that if I had nominated myself for any office, I would have won the elections. And this came true when I was elected as a member in the Palestinian Student Union at Oran

---

[12] Dweck SC. (2013). Ted Talk. The Power of yet.
https://video.search.yahoo.com/search/video?
India Tomorrow. (13 Jul 2014). 7 people commit suicide every day due to failure in examination
https://old.indiatomorrow.net/eng/7-people-commit-suicide-every-day-due-to-failure-in-examination

University. This event in my life increased my self-confidence tenfold and enabled me to face failure in my major.

Living in those circumstances, I decided to persist in the English Department and repeat the courses with some freshmen who joined the second semester. I brushed aside all advice from some friends urging me to join another Arabic major, like law or philosophy, where I would sleep all the semester and just take the exam in which success was guaranteed.

The Palestinian students at Oran University had developed a brotherhood and family like relationships because of the shared feeling while living in diaspora. We had lost our country, and this strengthened the bonds that tied us together. We sat and discussed our personal problems like brothers. I was one of the few students whose depression because of studies and family circumstances was reaching a dangerous level and my closest friends felt alarmed as I might suffer a nervous breakdown. Indeed, I was going through one of the most stressful periods in my life and my friends' sympathy and support was like a stick that helped an old frail man find his way. But I never considered any foolish action.

By the end of the second semester, I managed to pass one course but failed the others. That course was oral expression or conversational English and that was seen by everyone I knew as a great achievement considering that course was taught by a tough and stingy American professor. Prof Hoffman, who might be dead now, gave me a very constructive critique that I will never forget:

"You are a good speaker because you are not shy. Your main strength is that you are not suffering from language anxiety which draws a curtain over students and prevents them from talking. So well done. However, your English is still inaccurate in many places, and you still mispronounce, but this does not impede communication a lot. So, work hard on your grammar and your phonetics. Good luck."

Everyone I knew hailed that as a great victory because they had heard that Hoffman was really mean. In fact, that success in that course helped me dispel any thought of changing my English major. Later, Hoffman, who liked me, gripped my arm very tightly and said, "Stay here. Hang on, my son. Don't leave the English Department. You will make it."

I think the universe at that time collaborated to help me achieve my dream. I must admit that if I had failed with Hoffman, my destiny would have changed. I sometimes doubted that I did not deserve to pass but Hoffman saw something good in me and he took the right decision. That is proof that the grade 'I' or 'NY' can achieve more than the destructive 'F.'

However, repeated failures in writing expression played havoc on my psychology. I felt detained and deeply apprehensive that I might never be able to learn how to write in English because as one professor explained to us once the mistakes you make while learning in childhood become fossilised. When we asked about fossilisation, he explained that they become like rocks that are hard to break if they are not tackled in time. "That's it. I have become fossil fuels and my ridiculous English is like a rock that requires dynamite to destroy."

Chapter 8
The Wise Man Who Changed my Destiny

So, by June 1972, I had already wasted two years of my life since I left school in 1970. While almost all my peers were celebrating their success and they were sailing into their second or third year into their Arabic majors, I was standing here and all I possessed was a C in one course and a broken spirit. At that moment I stood at a crossroad; one direction was to stay in the English Department and continue to pursue my English dream at any cost, the second direction was to change my major at that point and go for an easy Arabic one. The third and most painful probability was to go back to Syria and explain my plight to my unsympathetic brothers, who would, in my experience, put all the blame on me and accuse me of being worthless, useless, smoking myself to death and a hooligan running after girls instead of studying. I excused my brothers because they had never joined university and they were utopians in the sense that if anyone joins university, he/she must pass with honours.

Although I had anticipated the outcome, I naively chose the third option. This was another blunder that I committed again. My brothers would not even listen to me and whenever they had a chance, they would repeat the same arguments and the same insults. They did not trust me at all.

I sometimes had the courage and protested. "I am not running after women. I am even too shy to talk to my female classmates. Am I introducing to you a new girlfriend everyday here?"

"Nonsense. Enough lying," one would comment.

"I spend the nights studying grammar and vocabulary. I am trying to memorise the 2,500,000 words in the English Arabic dictionary. I go to bed at three in the morning," I explained with bitterness.

As voices rose, my oldest brother, a born dictator would yell, "*Kul khara*! Eat shit. We have nothing here. Go back to Algeria, there is no other solution. End of conversation."

Apart from my second older brother who was sympathetic to my cause I was left alone in the arena wrestling with life. Because he had a meagre salary and he had just got married, he could not give me any financial support and all he could offer was sympathy and shelter. The problem was I needed money and my brothers were the only source of money for me.

Then one day, I had an idea. I approached a high official in the Palestinian embassy in Damascus known for his wisdom and generosity toward others. Because he knew my brother, he agreed to meet me. After granting me audience, I frankly requested a letter to the Algerian educational authorities asking them to give me a teaching position as a class teacher in a primary school. In those days, Algerian educational authorities in their intensive efforts to Arabise the nation, accepted school graduates from the Levant countries to teach Arabic, and maybe other subjects, at schools in the primary stage.

Having said that, he wanted to know why I wanted to teach and drop out of university. I explained my tragic situation in the English Department and my despair of my English dream. I briefed him on my brothers' abandonment of me. I told him that I was an orphan and spent all my teenage years in a military boarding school that resembled an orphanage. I told him that at least I could get a job with a small salary rather than wasting my time following a dream that will never come true. The official listened to me attentively and his body language and demeanour reflected sympathy to my cause. I ended by saying that studying English was like following a mirage.

He felt sorry for my suffering and bitterness and wondered at my brothers' harsh treatment.

"The mirage you are talking about is how you see things. There is no mirage. You have created it." Then he said something I always remember, "The problem is how you see the problem. You blame the world for your miserable situation." I looked at him with a question on my face.

"You blame your brothers, the school system, and the world that has abandoned you. And so on."

"What can I do?" I said in a pleading voice.

He adjusted his seat and looked me straight in the face.

"You must depend on yourself more. Forget about your brothers. You must have learnt the lesson, but you have not. Imagine that you had no brothers, what would you do? Besides, you should not have come back to Damascus, and you should not have ignored their previous messages to you. It seems they do not trust you and by putting this pressure on you, they believe they are doing you a favour."

I agreed.

"You do not seem to accept reality. Depend on yourself. Now Algeria gives you a scholarship and they do not penalise you for repeating. That is a blessing. There is nowhere in the world where a student is still accepted after repeated failure and his/her scholarship is running until they graduate. That is a lifetime chance. Do not let go. I repeat, do not let it go, my son. Millions of students dream of being in your position."

"I am doing my best, but I keep failing," I complained.

"No, you are not doing your best. You are not studying enough. You are keeping your problem to yourself. Do you ask your good classmates for help? Three words: I need help."

"Rarely. I feel ashamed of my mistakes, and I do not want to expose my disgraceful English."

"This is silly and a very negative attitude that is obstructing your progress. You must expose your weaknesses if you want to learn. You can learn from anyone if you want to. Do you know Socrates?"

"Yes, I do. I studied him, Plato, and Aristotle in the philosophy period in secondary school."

"Socrates, the wisest of the wisest, my son, said, 'Admitting one's ignorance is the first step in acquiring knowledge.'"

That was perhaps the greatest wisdoms I had ever heard. Truly, by hiding our ignorance we are condemning ourselves to failure.

"I do not know what to do. I am at a loss," I admitted.

"Take a classmate for coffee. Show your essays and ask for advice. Meet with your teacher and ask for more help. Meet with the head of the department and explain your situation. Have you done any if this?"

"Not really? I am not forceful, and I am shy when it comes to asking for help."

"Do not be shy to ask for help from anyone. We all need help sometimes. Talk about your weaknesses. Ask for an extra tuition from your teacher. And study nonstop until you catch up. And you will win."

"Do you think I should give up the idea of a job?" I asked reluctantly.

"Absolutely! If I give you that letter, I will condemn you to a low paid boring job and you will spend all your life fighting with kids. You will stagnate. Besides, one day the Algerian government will ask you where your university degree is and you will end up without a job. But when you get your bachelor's, one day you will think about a master's degree and maybe a doctorate. This is how you rise in the world. Go back and have one goal. No return until you get your bachelor's in the English language and literature." Then he paused and continued. "You know how respectable those holding such degrees are in our society. To me, they are equal to doctors. English is the most important language in the world." I nodded my head in bitterness and whispered, "I know."

He accompanied me to the door and put his hand on my shoulder. "Remember what the Prophet Muhammad said, *"The ink of the scholar is more important than the blood of the martyr."* And one day, you will devote your English to serving your Palestinian people's cause." Then he stretched out his hand and while holding my hand firmly said, "You are the maker of your future. Goodbye."

As I was leaving, he asked loud, "Do you have a return ticket to Algeria?" I nodded. Then wait a minute outside. "I want to talk to my secretary. Do not go."

As the secretary disappeared into that official office, I sat wondering about every word he said to me. I had never heard this before. I admitted that was the most important lecture in my life. This man is wisest of the wisest. Why didn't I meet him before as he could have saved me a lot of suffering? I wondered why my brothers did not talk to me like that.

In the middle of my deep thought, the secretary came out smiling and handed me an envelope. "His Excellency knows that you will need some money to get back to Algeria. So, he is lending you this amount and you will pay back when you graduate and get a job."

I felt overwhelmed. I felt some tears streaming down my cheeks when the gentle secretary handed me a tissue putting her hand on my shoulder. That man was so nice that he did not give me the money directly to avoid embarrassing me.

That was a major turning point in my life. That great man boosted my morale, sharpened my enthusiasm, and pulled me out of that deep hole I was falling in. At least he talked me out of that silly idea to get a teaching job. Now, I announced to the world that I was born again. I wanted to go back to that man and kiss his hand and assure him that I will be more faithful to him than his own son, and definitely will pay back the money he had given me. Above all, I will take an oath that I will use my English as a weapon to liberate my occupied country as he requested. And neither the UK nor the USA nor the UN can sanction me from using English as a weapon because it is not a Weapon of Mass Destruction. Indeed, it is a *Weapon of Mass Construction*.

As I stood on the pavement waiting for the bus, I inhaled and exhaled and felt I was breathing and alive for the first time. Before meeting this wise man, I had felt lifeless. That wise man had given me the most invaluable lesson in life. I felt like a sick person who had just been given a prescription for how to heal and recover. The prescription was to trust in God, depend on yourself, ask for help, be less submissive and more aggressive, admit ignorance, ignore your silly self-pride, and keep studying day and night until you stand on your feet ready to compete. For the first time in years, I was smiling to myself, and I was beginning to see the world around me from a different perspective. I took a vow to defeat the language of the most powerful country in the world.

"No return until you get your bachelor's in English Literature." His words echoed in my ears.

Chapter 9
Defeating the English Language

As I emerged from the airplane after landing at Algiers Airport, I was excited, and I felt I was returning home. I even imagined the whole teaching staff and students of the English Department were waiting for me at the airport on a red carpet. I thanked God for his mercy and for guiding me to meet that official at the embassy who provided me with a new heart, a new brain, and a fresh perspective on the world around me. My mother Hamda's prayer had been answered again as she used to pray every morning at dawn, "Ghassoub, Son of Hamda, I pray to God that he sends you the most sympathetic people in the world. Ameen." And he did. The official, the wise man at the Palestinian Embassy in Damascus was one of those people.

Now it was the year 1972, and I was at Oran university, in the English section, sitting in class waiting for the professor to begin the semester. I was sitting with the third generation of school graduates as my classmates from year ago were already in their second year. Now I was again a freshman starting from zero and as the Arab proverb goes 'God forgive what has been done, and what has gone, and we are today the children of today.'

Although the new students were four or five years younger than me, I felt for the first time a feeling of belonging to the English Department, I felt like I was not an alien or a guest but a host to these new students. So, for the first time in my history in this section I sat in the front and not in the back. I was determined not to be passive anymore, nor to be a day dreamer and nor of a classroom sleeper. Those were things of the past.

When I sat in the front seat in class, I wanted to send a message to everyone that I am not sitting in the back of the English wagon as a passenger, or a hitchhiker being offered a lift. Never, my message was that I am driving the English wagon and all of you are passengers. From day one, I made it a habit that I always arrived early to class and waited for the teacher and other students to arrive. That boosted my self-confidence and projected me as a leader and not as a follower.

As new students began to arrive, I smiled at each and said 'hi,' 'hello,' something I had not done before. I felt that behaviour gave me more self-confidence and a sense of possession of the classroom. Then the door opened and a short, dark boy, wearing jeans, with the most beautiful smile on his face came straight to sit next to me. He stretched out his hand enthusiastically and gave me a strong handshake, one of the strongest handshakes I had ever had. He said, "Firnas."

"Ghassoub, you can call me Mustafa," I said. I was taken aback a little by Firnas and his directness. I wondered why he chose to sit next to me. Perhaps that was a good omen and Firnas might be one of those who heard my mother's prayers.

By that time, the professor had already entered, and the first session started. During the session, I made myself focus. I participated whenever I was sure of the point and listened carefully. For the first time, a teacher would comment on my answer positively. I felt elated, flattered and I was in the heart of the English Department.

Firnas, just a simple secondary school graduate, was a surprise to everyone. He spoke English fluently, accurately and with confidence. His comments were very interesting, and he showed deeper thinking. Everyone was impressed, especially the teacher.

When we stood outside after the session, Firnas was happy in my company, and we quickly broke the ice. I handed him a cigarette and he was so thankful as he did not have any. This was the beginning of a sincere friendship and I had just befriended the best student in the English Department. We became friends and study buddies. He even moved to a room in the same building where I lived. The world was conspiring on my behalf now.

Firnas and I had an agreement; we decided to communicate in English as much as we could outside the classroom. I told him not to hesitate to correct me and he did. He used to look at my essays and help me to correct mistakes, then by the time I handed it to the teacher, it was already a kind of a second draft rather than first. Firnas and I used to hold debates about issues we read or heard in the room or as we were wandering around the university. We even discussed the Palestinian cause in English which helped me acquire vocabulary and political expressions. In a matter of months, I had made great progress in English at the speed of a lightning, which had been noticed by teachers. Their positive comments motivated me to study harder on my own.

Now I felt I was catching up with Firnas's level and he noticed it. Firnas came from a poor background from the countryside, and I was pleased to provide him with cigarettes and pay for his coffee any time we happened to be together. He was grateful for that, and he spared no efforts to help me improve my English.

I was astonished at how fast I was progressing in all the language skills. This was due to the motivation which that official in the Embassy, the *Aristotle of Palestine*, as I nicknamed him, had injected in me and, of course, Firnas's friendship.

At the end of the semester, I passed all courses and I said adieu to the 'I' or 'not yet' grade. This was something from the past. My grades were just above C but in oral expression I started getting Bs. One day Firnas, whose grades ranged between As and B+s, joked that I was at his heels and soon would overtake him. He did not feel jealous at all and considered me more than a brother. I enjoyed Firnas's company, sense of humour, and simplicity.

Reminiscing about Firnas's episode in my life, I conclude that individuals play dramatic roles in each other's lives. The chemistry between me and Firnas from the moment he entered the classroom for the first time at the beginning of the semester was so obvious that the observer would think that these two individuals had known each other for a long time. Firnas in other words, was an intervention force that appeared at the most crucial moment in my academic life. "*When you want something, the whole universe unites to help you achieve it.*" I turned my face toward heaven and read a verse from the Holy Quran for my mother's soul and thanked her for her prayers.

The one-thousand-mile trip starts with one step. Having completed my first semester after two attempts, I had just started my one-thousand-mile journey into the English language. As I stepped into the second semester with confidence and enthusiasm, I realised we were navigating into a new world. In addition to studying grammar, oral and written expressions, I had to launch into studying something called phonetics. I had zero knowledge of this subject. As we were registering into the second semester course, nobody could uncover that mysterious course. I felt apprehensive like others and was full of expectations. I was flying with colours in the English language atmosphere, and this so-called phonetics could be a storm. "I will watch for it and will not let it interrupt my flight." I assured myself that there will be other forces that will collaborate with me against any unexpected enemies.

The teacher who came to teach us that course, was to our surprise, a Frenchman and not a native speaker of English. He was tall, good looking and well dressed. He was very sophisticated. He was very friendly and from day one managed to dispel our fears and replace them with assurance and tranquillity. He explained that the course was about phonetics which would teach us the standard pronunciation of English words. He had a PhD in phonetics and from day one we decided to nickname him *Doctor Phonetics.*

Dr. Phonetics said that we had to learn the International Phonetic Alphabet (IPA). Hearing that, I panicked as I was barely able to learn English and had no room in my brain for another language. He gave us some handouts and the new alphabet looked like an ancient language. Those symbols show you how to pronounce the word and they are written between two slashes after each word in the English Dictionary. Suddenly, I had discovered a treasure.

After having mastered those symbols, I realised that I was becoming more independent, and I could pronounce any word in English on my own. Although the process of internalising those phonetic symbols was often agonising, they proved to be one of the most useful tools to helping me learn the English language independently. For example, words like 'chaos, conscientious, colonel, choir, etc., became no mystery to me and I could pronounce them with confidence. The system even shows where to place the stress on words. Learning IPA increased my self-confidence dramatically.

Phonetics was entirely about how we articulate sounds. Dr. Phonetics immersed us in an ocean of jargon that we had to use to describe the speech organs and how they function in producing sounds. I found myself struggling with jargon like bilabial, alveolar, labiodental etc. I once asked if we had to study Latin, and everybody laughed. But the fact is, the phonetic symbols are based on Latin. Dr. Phonetics did his best to explain how we articulate sounds. But the most useful was his demonstration. We were fascinated by the way he articulated sounds and we all imitated him. Although he was a non-native speaker of English, he had one of the best pronunciations I had ever heard. And now, I attributed most of my success in redressing my pronunciation to Dr. Phonetics. His patience, professionalism, and sense of humour made him a great model.

Talking about sound articulation, Dr. Phonetics divided the English sounds into two categories; one called voiced, the second called voiceless. The only two sounds I had struggled with were the 'b' and 'p'. This is because Arabic does not include the letter 'p' and all 'p's are pronounced as 'b's. So: paper, piper, Pepsi are pronounced as *baber, biber, bebsi.* That was really funny. It was very embarrassing when I was caught by teachers or students pronouncing p as b. Algerian classmates did not have this problem because they studied French from an early age. In fact, French was their first language, and Arabic was their third or fourth language.

Dr. Phonetics showed us a technique to distinguish between 'p' and the 'b' properly. He held a piece of paper in front of his mouth and when he produced the 'b' sound nothing happened, the paper stood still. But when he produced the 'p' sound, the piece of paper was blown and shaken by the little gust of wind produced from the lips. He explained that the 'p' is a voiceless sound and air is released from the mouth when you pronounce it. However, the 'b' is silent, and no air is produced.

I commented, "With the 'P', there is an explosion. Be careful." Everybody laughed and Dr. Phonetics nodded his head in agreement and said that was nearly the right word. This helped me overcome my poor pronunciation. It also became one of my funny parts in my sessions when I became a teacher. Dr. Phonetics' techniques became essential parts of my methodology while I was teaching English to Arab students. I admit I owe Dr. Phonetics a heavy debt of gratitude.

But I hated the second group, the *vowels*, and I called them the evil group. I suffered while trying to distinguish between the 'i' and the 'e', the 'o' and the 'u', etc. I suffered on two levels: pronunciation and spelling. For example, I could not understand the complicated difference between saying and writing the words 'cup' and 'cop'. Even after four decades of teaching English, I still make mistakes in vowels and remind myself of words I am going to spell on the board. For example, I still try to keep in mind the difference between 'crises' and 'crisis'. English vowels are one of the most troublesome aspects of learning the English language for Arab learners, especially those from the Levant.

One of the most fearsome tests given by Dr. Phonetics was when he stood in front of us reading a paragraph at almost normal speed and we had to transcribe what he said in IPA. He used to repeat a phrase or a sentence twice and pause a little, then move on. I used to panic and leave a space when I missed something then come back at the end of the test to fill in the space with whatever I could remember. Sometimes, I remembered nothing. That was one of the most challenging parts in my English language *journey*, or in my *war* with English.

In the semester that followed, I do not remember exactly but another phonetics teacher one day said, "Let's go to the language lab." We all wondered what a language lab was.

"Are we going to mix vowels with consonants into a flask? What liquid are we going to add to the mixture?" we joked.

The lab contained around 25 booths with glass partitions and a big desk for the professor monitoring at the front. Each booth was equipped with headphones and a tape-recorder fixed in the desk. As we sat, the professor gave each an audio cassette and he said that we would be on our own during the semester.

The session consisted of two parts. In one part, we would wear our headphones and repeat after him so we could learn how to pronounce some difficult words. In the second part, we would work on our own, at our own pace. The cassette contained short audio passages that we would listen to and imitate, then record and listen to ourselves.

The professor monitored and listened to each student and interrupted to correct or make comments on our pronunciation in terms of stress, pitch, clarity, and even accent. I took that seriously and imitated the speaker on the tape very well. The speaker was a native speaker and spoke standard English, or BBC English, or Queen's English as these varieties were referred to.

From time to time, the professor would interrupt me to correct or make some comments. But once, the British teacher interrupted to say, "Ghassoub, you are doing very well. When I listen to you now, I feel someone British is talking. You are even getting the accent. Well done. Keep it up." Hearing that, I felt over the moon and almost sprang on my feet. I felt really flattered when that "teacher" mentioned this in front of some students later. Some classmates felt jealous. Exactly as Charlotte had anticipated, around 15 years before, by the Dead Sea. "You will be a British gentleman." There might be some exaggeration here, but I was working so hard to speak an accent-less English.

The language lab experience was a great episode in my struggle to *master*, or a better word to *defeat*, the English language. It perfected my pronunciation and helped me to get rid of my accent gradually until I began to speak a form of RP, Received Pronunciation. According to Dr. Phonetics, this is the form used by the BBC radio announcers. I was lucky to use the language lab because later it was closed as it was costly as the Department got bigger. Then it became something of the past. I must admit that the lab was very helpful.

The other novelty we experienced in another semester was a new course, Introduction to Literature. Because I had enjoyed studying Arabic literature at school in the past and I loved reading, I transferred that passion to English literature. However, I must admit that I found authentic English in that literature extremely difficult to understand. My poor Longman dictionary of contemporary English was exhausted from being overused on those long, lonely nights as I was struggling to understand Shakespeare and Chaucer. I sometimes cursed Shakespeare and doubted that he was writing in English. I wondered why he had to write his plays in such a strange language. "Why use the archaic word 'Knave' when you can easily say instead 'dishonest.'" I felt distressed whenever I came to grapple with Shakespeare, and this reminded me of the early sad days in my battle against the English language. But I reminded myself of what Buddha said, "If you cannot handle stress, you cannot handle success."

The most daunting task was when we were asked to do some discourse analysis and look for the deeper meaning of a text, which I got wrong on many occasions. I sometimes argued that I reserve the right to interpret the meaning the way I understand it. Some teachers were flexible, and some insisted on one meaning. In fact, I always managed to get a pass and thanked God for his support. Although I enjoyed some English poetry, I thought that Arabic poetry was superior because of its great rhythm and rhyme. When I recited English poetry, very often I did not distinguish between prose and poetry.

For the next two years until graduation, we alternated between British literature, American literature, British civilisation, and American civilisation. Only once we studied Anglo African literature. During break time, some patriotic Algerian students argued that that our English curriculum was camouflaged by the word civilisation and literature, when instead it was a new cultural invasion. I had reservations on that position, and I argued that literature and civilisation were an integral part of any profound study of any language. So, there were no evil intentions.

This became a hot potato and professors got involved in the debate. Finally, they said that they did not know any other literature to teach. I regretted that no one had thought about doing some kind of contrastive analysis between Arabic and English literature. Arabic was looked down upon those days.

In the second year, I had to study a second language and I was given a choice between Spanish and Russian. I chose Spanish but for administrative reasons I could not join the course and I had to take Russian. The Iraqi lady who taught the course was very intelligent, focused, and she loved the language. Sometimes she would spend most of the time talking about the Russian culture in English rather than teaching the language. She even let us listen to the Soviet Union national anthem and we repeated the words. We suspected that she was a communist agent and, unfortunately, we did not learn very much. We wondered whether she was spreading the communist philosophy and we did not take learning Russian seriously. All we had achieved was leaning some vocabulary, the numbers 1-10, and a few expressions.

In the last semester, we were told that we were going to study TEFL. When I heard that acronym for the first time, I smiled to myself because the word 'tefl' means coffee grounds in Arabic. In Palestinian Jordanian culture, the amounts of 'tefl' and 'animal bones' that are found outside your house gate determine how hospitable and generous you are. When I explained this to the teacher and fellow classmates, they burst out laughing. "So, if the ground outside my house gate is clean, does this indicate that I am mean?" one student asked. "In the Bedouin philosophy, yes," I responded.

One thing distinguished the English Department at Oran University, and that was the relaxed, friendly, and cosy atmosphere that dominated the sessions. We also had small numbers in the sections which encouraged more interaction among ourselves and the professors. You could tell jokes and stories without hesitation.

The professor, Harry, an American from South Carolina, was one of the funniest people I had ever met. His sense of humour was unmatched in the English Department. After telling my anecdote about 'tefl,' Harry said, "This is an interesting way of starting this course. However, 'Tefl' in Jordan means coffee grounds, but here at the English Department it means something else. TEFL stands for Teaching English as a Foreign Language," he said with a big smile on his face. An 'aha…' went through the class. This was the first time in my life I heard about this. It was the year 1975 and my saga with *teaching* English as a foreign language had just started.

"That was a nice way to start the session. Thank you for that little anecdote about tefl and coffee grounds. It was a good way to start and break the ice," Harry said to me after class.

"Really. In fact, I was a bit worried that I had distracted the students' attention by telling that silly anecdote. I was going to apologise," I commented.

"No, not at all. Just the opposite. Here is a golden rule for you as a future teacher. If you start the session with something funny, strange, or gripping, this will hook the students' attention," he said.

"Interesting. That is true. I realised the students paid more attention to you and looked at you curiously," I added.

"Exactly. You are a good observer. Your coffee grounds anecdote was especially useful," he reiterated.

"I will keep this advice in my mind. 'Make the beginning gripping,'" I concluded.

TEFL was an interesting course because of Harry. He was resourceful, funny, exciting, and very friendly. He was like a great master, and we were 10 or 12 faithful disciples. I, personally, watched his every move in class, listened to every word he said, and copied his body language. I reasoned with myself, "If Harry has been able to capture our attention with his teaching strategies here, I will be able to achieve that if I use them with my future learners, of course with some modifications." Harry's TEFL's sessions had been fascinating all through the course. In retrospect, Harry made me and most of us think seriously about teaching English as a future career.

Another factor that made Harry's session more lovable was that we did not take exams. For the first time, we were going to suffer less exam anxiety. Harry had announced a few weeks before the end of the final semester that our graduation project in TEFL would be to teach an English class to classmates. He added that he wanted us to teach a real class in schools, but that was not feasible at that time. Hearing that, we all applauded and shouted 'hurray.'

"I understand this euphoria," he said with a broad smile.

After that, he provided us with a detailed guideline and the assessment criteria. The guidelines stated that one can teach any aspect of the language like vocabulary, grammar, reading etc. However, the main constraint and the most challenging requirement was that the session should not exceed 10 minutes. In other words, within 10 minutes you must give a complete lesson that includes all the parts from A to Z. That was going to be very challenging.

I panicked and felt very nervous. This would be my first teaching session and wondered how I could present a complete session that includes a beginning, development and an ending as Harry usually did, within 10 minutes. As I had a few weeks ahead of me, I spent some sleepless nights thinking about what to teach. Finally, and after a lot of hesitation and reasoning with myself, I decided to teach grammar. I chose the *Active and the Passive voice.*

Because of my poor English when I joined the English Department years back, or more precisely when I started my war with English, I swore to memorise English grammar believing that good knowledge of grammar would improve my productive skills, i.e., speaking and writing. Unfortunately, this turned to be untrue. This is the fallacy that many teachers and students have. Knowing grammar rules does not necessarily mean better productive skills. However, my deep knowledge of grammar had paid off and I did not waste my time. I could teach the passive voice or any other grammatical topic with ease.

In those days, we had no internet, and few resources were available, so we had to depend on the limited number of books available in the Departmental library. Besides, we had to create our own teaching material. As I needed some flash cards, some drawings and some pictures for illustration and elicitation, I asked some friends, who had some drawing skill, to sketch, for example, a broken window, a broken vase, a torn book and so on. Having done all that, I felt satisfied with my realia for the session. Then I prepared a truly short written exercise. Work sheets had to be written by hand as I could not obtain a typewriter, and if I did, I was so slow in typing. I drafted my lesson plan several times until I produced my final version of my lesson plan that I had to submit to Harry a week before the actual session.

My plan, I remember looked like this:

Objective: passive; simple present and past
Audience: Arab students. intermediate English learners – poor passive voice use
Material: drawings, flash cards, handouts.
Time: 10 minutes
Activities
Introduction – gripping.
Oral activities
Written
Group work
Homework
Round off

Having finalised my lesson plan, I submitted it with confidence. Now with all my material ready, and the plan clear in my head, I overcame all fears and panic. I kept rehearsing the lesson alone in my room, then suddenly I had an idea. I gathered a few friends and practiced teaching the passive voice. They were indeed very poor in grammar and the plan worked. That was fun and they gave some feedback which helped me improve the delivery.

Then it was the day of the lesson. A few students had presented their mini lessons before me, and they were not very impressive. They did not show enthusiasm and were extremely nervous. One of them did not even have any material which revealed he was not well prepared. Harry gave feedback immediately after the session and he also involved the audience in giving their reflections on the session. He was direct and honest in his evaluation.

Then, "Mustafa. It's your call," Harry said.

I felt my heart pounding hard and I thought the whole class could hear my heart beats. It was like a drum beating inside my chest. I sprang to my feet, moved to the front with confidence, and stood looking at my classmates and Harry who was sitting in the back. I smiled as I was trying to hide my nervousness.

At that moment, I remembered my father back in the village, 15 years ago, when I was only a child, telling me to carry my book, stand in the front of the room and read that poem loud. He would yell, "This is not loud enough. Why is your head down? That is not good. Repeat with gusto. Come on. Read loud. Look at me here."

Today, "I will just do that, Dad. I will not disappoint you," I said to myself.

The lesson timing started, and the professor gave me a nod to begin.

"When I was a child of five years old, one day I broke a beautiful vase. One of my mom's favourites. When my mother returned home, she asked me who broke the vase, I said, 'I did', with a trembling voice."

I paused and looked at my audience who looked interested and wanted to know what happened.

"Can you guess what she did?" I asked the audience and waited.

"She caressed your hair and told you to be careful," one said.

"She yelled at you and threatened to tell your father," another said laughing.

"So tell us. What did your mother do?" one asked impatiently.

"She smacked me, twisted my ear, and told me that we were not millionaires and how the hell could she replace such a beautiful vase."

"Oh! Poor Mustafa! Your mom shouldn't have been that harsh. It's only a vase!" some girls said.

I actually acted the scene with my mother in somehow slow motion; how she smacked, how I reacted and the pain I felt when she twisted my ear, etc. The audience were charmed by the mini play taking place in front of them. That introduction took no more than one minute, but it served my purpose. I hooked the audience and now I had them in my hand.

"Today I am going to teach you a strategy that helps you avoid saying 'I did' when you commit a sin which saves you from your parents' wrath, I mean anger…anger." I remembered the word 'wrath' from a movie I had seen earlier, 'Grapes of Wrath'. I mentioned that word deliberately to teach new vocabulary, and to impress. This statement also motivated them more.

"Now, I am going to teach you how to use the clever, devious, passive voice and to avoid the stupid naive active voice." This stimulated more laughter and personified the active and passive. Now the students were active and engaged. I had achieved my first aim. For the next eight minutes, I turned the class into a hive of activity. I engaged every student in the group. I put them in pairs, and in groups to do something. I set a written exercise and gave feedback. Finally, I used the pictures and flash cards for enhancement of the passive. I complimented the students when they answered. *'The glass was broken.' 'The wallet was stolen.'* And so on…Finally, I ended by summarising the main points and assigning a small homework task. Harry and the audience broke into loud applause. No standing ovation. Ten minutes exactly and I had covered all the session's objectives.

Harry, who had not left his seat to give feedback on previous student-teachers but did it while seated, now stood up and came to the front. I was surprised.

"What do you think?" he asked the audience.

"Great. Fantastic. Well done," some boys and girls shouted.

"Yes, fantastic. Well done, Mustafa. You have really implemented all the strategies that this course has preached. Look you are going to be a great TEFL, *not coffee grounds*, teacher." This stimulated more laughter and applause.

"But I want to say something. Mustafa, you are more of an actor, and acting is a very useful tool to demonstrate and explain whatever you want. Acting is the best method to teach."

He paused then said, "You have given a great session. Good luck."

Harry's prediction came true, and I became a successful TEFL teacher.

I felt so proud of Harry and my classmates' evaluation of my ever first teaching session. I had already been very popular among all I knew, and this made me more popular. I became a star. They marvelled at the little story, the attention grabber, but they were not sure whether it was true or that I had made it up. I told them that we were poor and all we had were some primitive clay containers to store our olive oil and other staple foods.

Perfect preparation prevents failure. One of the most valuable lessons I learnt from that experience was that the more you prepare the more success you will achieve, and the opposite is a recipe for failure. Some of the classmates that day gave lousy lessons and received poor feedback because it was obvious, they prepared little and did not take it seriously. From that moment, *'prior perfect preparation'* became one of my mottos in life and one of the secrets of my success as a teacher.

So, always remember the *Golden* **6 Ps**: **P**rior **P**erfect **P**reparation **P**revents **P**oor **P**erformance.

Hard to believe, in a matter of three years, I rose from a miserable beginner in the English language to an actor on the stage in English, and from a forgotten Palestinian to be crowned as the American dream. How did all that happen? The story of the American dream started when the American literature teacher told us that our group would be performing the American dream play in the university theatre, if we all agreed. That was a surprise and we all agreed at once. As we read and analysed the play, I was selected to play the American dream role.

Although I did not comprehend the plot of the American dream very well, I was given the script of my role that I had to memorise. I acted that good looking young man, but hollow inside, who is adopted by an old couple who cared about the exterior and ignored the interior. I understood that very well. However, the most important thing to me was that I was acting in an American play and performing in English. I thought I was dreaming.

We performed the play in the main auditorium at the university and we had a big audience. Some Palestinian friends who attended the performance said, "The English Section did not only train you how to be a teacher, but how to be an actor as well. Are they sending you to Hollywood next?"

Anther commented, "Perhaps there they might think that Ghassoub Sharif is Omar Sharif's brother."

Chapter 10
From the American Dream to a Nation that Will Not Die

The success of the American dream play prompted some Palestinian students at Oran University, including me, to perform a play about Palestine's tragedy. So, four of us met with Yousuf, a mature law student. Yusuf was much older than us, with an artificial leg, and he had been a resident of one of the refugee camps in Jordan. He repeatedly urged us to perform a play about Palestine. He claimed that he had a script from his school days, and said he even participated in directing the play. We did not take him seriously and joked about his claims of being a play director.

As we entered his room, Yousuf was resting on his bed. He had removed his artificial leg and laid it next to him on his bed. He was always smiling and laughing and we used to call him uncle as he was years older than most of us. Yusuf was a man of two extremes; he had a great sense of humour, and unfortunately a very bad temper. One day, a weird friend of ours said something disgraceful about his leg that made Yousuf throw his artificial leg at him. We all panicked.

"Hello, the American Dream," Yousuf yelled as soon as he saw me. I was nicknamed the American Dream. I liked that.

"Uncle. So, you have seen the American dream?" I asked him.

"Yes. You really played well, and you should give up the idea of teaching and think of a career in Holy Wood." We all burst out laughing. I should have taken that advice seriously.

"No. I am not joking. I am serious. You now speak good English, and you are good looking with those rare blue eyes. You are even acquiring a kind of British accent. True you are rather short, but you are qualified to act in Holy

Wood. The Omar Sharif of Palestine," he said with an amazing glow in his big eyes.

I hugged him and kissed his cheek as I usually did. I loved Yousuf and I used to spend time with him in his room helping him when he took off his leg. That gave me great pleasure.

"Uncle. We know you are one of Ghassoub's fans. But now we are coming to discuss that play that you had suggested before. What do you call it?" one friend shouted.

Hearing this, Yousuf dropped whatever was in his hand, adjusted his position, paused, looked at us with a very big smile as if preparing himself for a speech.

"Oh! You look serious this time. So, now it is time to do business. You mean now you are finally convinced to perform a play about our beloved Palestine, about 'the nation that will not die,'" he said with a sparkle in his wide eyes. Perhaps the widest eyes I had ever seen. But scary sometimes.

"Yes. We want to perform the nation that will not die," we said in unison like a group of children and broke into loud laughter.

"So, the play's title is: *The Nation that will not Die, Uncle*?" one asked.

"Yes, dear," he replied.

"Great title," I commented.

All nodded in agreement.

"Let's go for it," we all shouted enthusiastically.

With his left artificial leg resting on his bed, the uncle called, "Ghass!" (That is what he called me sometimes.) "Open that suitcase in the corner and hand me that thick booklet."

"That's the hidden treasure then, uncle! Are you hiding a gun or something else there as well?" we joked.

"If I did, the Genies would not be able to find it," he said gazing at us. We felt scared. The uncle had fought in real battles in the past. That is why he has one leg only.

Just three months after that very first meeting with Yousuf, the Great Uncle, I and some Palestinian students were standing at the university's main entrance distributing coloured leaflets inviting students, staff, and their families to attend a Palestinian play to be performed by students. We were handing out leaflets in three languages, the ones spoken at university: French, Arabic, and English. We tried our best to campaign for the play.

The leaflets gave a synopsis of the play. It went something like this: "This play presents the tragedy of the Palestinian people and their daily suffering at the hands of the Israeli occupation authorities. This nation has vowed to resist and not to surrender."

I took advantage of both my knowledge of English and French to promote the play among university staff who spoke those two languages. Faculty at the English Institute were very supportive and listened passionately despite their sympathy for Israel.

The Algerian Authorities were very supportive of any political activity anywhere in the country that Palestinian students wanted to do. They gave us *carte blanche*. For this play, they lent us military uniforms and real weapons, which was astonishing, but no ammunition of course, and they gave us permission to perform in the main auditorium at the university.

I played the principal role of an Israeli colonel who was the subject of fun all the time. From the American dream to an Israeli colonel. Students wondered what was next. Maybe an Israeli prime minister as the joke went around. I was given that role due to my physical appearance and to my military upbringing at the military boarding school where I had spent seven years doing daily military marches and living a quasi-military lifestyle. So, I was qualified for that. As we failed to get any females to act in the play, some boys volunteered to do that.

Of course, Yousuf was the undisputed director. He declared from day one that he was the absolute authority, or he threatened to withdraw. We had to accept. Yousuf used to remind us, "Too many cooks spoil the food." We agreed.

As we stood facing him, he gazed at us and said, "Disobedience means expulsion."

I shouted, "It means more than that: death."

Yousuf became the absolute ruler. Perhaps, that was one of the main secrets of our success.

The auditorium was packed with staff, students, and many guests. Even though the play would be performed in standard Arabic, many non-Arabic speaking staff decided to attend due to our intensive promotion campaign that aroused their curiosity. Besides, there had been many sympathizers among them. We also managed to get volunteers from the Algerian community to sit among the non-Arabic speaking audience and give some live interpretation of the scenes, which worked well.

Our first performance was highly successful, and we received a standing ovation from the audience. Everybody was impressed by this bunch of students who had no acting experience at all but managed to give such an impressive performance. They all praised my performance in particular, and some said I made them hate Israelis because I acted my role well. "But do not hate me," I begged.

Yousuf was very proud, and we thanked him and attributed this success to his strong leadership. We had worked so hard that our efforts had paid off to the point where Oran's local authorities invited us to repeat the play at the Opera House in the city. That was unbelievable and we had never predicted that because the Opera House was only for professional actors.

We were in disbelief when we learnt that many officers and soldiers would attend the play. I even felt nervous in case those military personnel might mock my performance as a colonel in the army. We thought that we might become so famous that the President of the Republic would appear at the door any minute. We comforted each other by saying that we were just simple students, not professional actors, and it is forgivable if we make mistakes.

"We are trying to present our tragedy to the world that has turned its back on us."

The Opera's three floors were packed. Just an hour before going on stage and as we were behind the screens, something crazy happened. Hilal Sabah, a close friend and the one who plays the role of a Palestinian commando, a freedom fighter in our perspective, but a terrorist in the Israeli perspective, came and whispered something shocking in my ear.

"Look. You know the scene when you are interrogating and torturing me then I pretend to spit on you, then you slap me hard, and I pretend to fall on the floor?" he asked.

"Yes, I know. Why are you asking now?" I replied.

"Listen. I am planning to gather as much saliva in my mouth as possible, and then spit that on your face directly. It will be real. You know that stuff will land on your cheek, nose, anywhere on your face. It will be the biggest spit in your life. Man! Let us make the scene real and exciting. We are in the Opera House, man! This does not happen every day," he said with the most sarcastic smile on his face.

I could not believe what Hilal was saying. I knew Hilal was stubborn, funny and would do anything to play a trick for a laugh.

With a shock on my face, I said, "Are you crazy?" Then I continued, "In this case, I will gather all my strength, you know I am strong, and will give you a real slap, the toughest slap in your life which will send you rolling down on to the stage. I warn you. Do not do it. You will regret it. My slap may cause you a hearing loss," I said looking at him squarely trying to scare him. I knew he would do it.

"Go to hell. I do not care. Do whatever you want." He giggled.

As the play started, I got so excited that I forgot every word that Hilal had said. When we came to the scene which Hilal mentioned, as I was yelling and cursing terrorists and Palestinians, gazing at Hilal who was acting as a Palestinian fighter, Hilal executed his plan and spat a mouthful of saliva in my face. For a moment, I thought he was acting as normal, but as I touched that disgusting stuff on my face, I landed the toughest slap on his face which literally sent him rolling off the chair as I had warned earlier. This made the audience clap hard and boo me. That turned out to be the best scene in the play.

At the end of the play, we received a grand standing ovation. Hilal and I kept joking and telling each other how it felt. Many people came and shook hands and we felt like great stars. For months to come, certain people, when they saw me in the street, would pause and say, "Ah. That is Colonel Benyamin." I began to feel worried as Algerians hated Jews.

The Palestinian Consul congratulated us, and he said every Palestinian was proud of us. He turned to me and said, "I will recommend that they take you into a future Palestinian army as a captain."

For months to come, professors and students at the department kept asking about the play. They wondered how we had succeeded in giving such a performance although we were just students and amateurs. I answered by saying, "When you are being burned at the stake, you do not fake pain. It is real. We were not acting, but we were demonstrating to the world how it feels to live under occupation and to be homeless, or countryless. Acting in that play was a demonstration of our real emotions. We are seeking justice."

One day, a British professor invited me to talk to the students about the play during the session. That would be my first lecture in English to an audience about Palestine. Now, as that wise official at the embassy in Damascus, the Aristotle of Palestine, had predicted some years before, "Your English will serve your cause." And here I am, using my English as a weapon to liberate Palestine. No one can seize this weapon from me because it is not a Weapon of Mass Destruction. Rather, English is a *Weapon of Mass Attraction*.

Chapter 11
The English Word is Mightier than the Sword

I have never done any field research on why individuals study a foreign language. But we know most of us study a language to pursue a major in that language, or to have a career in that language, and so on. I studied English because of the passion that resulted from meeting certain individuals. Ultimately English would help me make a living.

I realised that my English became a political platform to present my oppressed people's plight to the world. If I wanted to calculate the amount of talking, I did in English through my university years and afterwards, I would discover that more than 50 percent was spent on the Palestinian issue and international politics. Of course, you should stay away from domestic politics if you live in the Middle East. My obsession with politics resulted from my upbringing and the close companionship with my father when I was a child. He was really obsessed with politics. Having no brothers or sisters to play with around the house, my parents became my whole universe at home.

My father, who deserves a whole book to be written about him, shaped my outlook and my personality. In the '50s when I was a child, he used to spend hours by his old radio listening to the Voice of Arabs, from Cairo, the BBC Arabic radio from London, and even to Israel's radio sometimes. The radio was such a novelty in that era that only a few families possessed it in the village, and everyone wondered about that magical box. My father would never miss the news bulletin and of course I sat next to him most of the time. Having suffered bad hearing loss, he would sit so close to the radio and even put his ear too close to the speaker. Sometimes, if he missed something, he would ask me to repeat.

The funny thing was I repeated things that I did not understand. However, I was so excited to discover that magical box and always wondered 'how those announcers and actors managed to fit their huge bodies in that small box that could contain only a few small sparrows'!

During the '50s, some major events rocked the Middle East like the nationalisation of the Suez Canal and the subsequent tripartite aggression on Egypt by UK, France and Israel. The most shocking of all was that Israel managed within only 10 years to be part of an international military alliance. My father used to curse and get mad at the news. Sometimes, he used to listen to the news with some of his peers surrounding him, which would always lead to a hot debate and a verbal battle ensued. I felt amused at older people insulting each other when they disagreed. At 8, I was familiar with the most hated figure, David Ben Gurion, the first Israeli prime minister and the founder of Israel.

Growing up in such an environment, and my deep feeling of the injustice that had been inflicted on my people, politicised me from an early age. I got so involved in discussing politics that it became the only topic I would discuss with others. Thus, English and later French became my weapons to fight for the usurped rights of my people. Speakers of these two languages had shown enough understanding and adequate tolerance that I had rarely entered into a verbal battle with anyone, and discussion always ended on a friendly note and a desire on both sides to continue the discussion.

However, talking politics in Arabic has been a depressing experience. Sad to say, many Arab people from the Atlantic Ocean to the Arabian Gulf, have little tolerance toward anyone that contradicts their political point of view. One day, an Arab threatened to hit me with his shoe because I was critical of his country's president. This explains the throwing of both shoes by an Iraqi Journalist at George Bush, the American President, during a press conference with the Iraqi President in 2008. Throwing a shoe or waving a shoe at someone is considered the biggest offence in our culture.

But the most shocking experience in this sense I had, took place while I was talking politics with some colleagues at the college where I worked. Those colleagues came from diverse backgrounds. Of course, I was talking in English. While I was talking, another Palestinian, who was eating at a nearby table and could hear my speech, suddenly came to me, looked me straight in the face and said slowly and clearly, "You are a traitor, you are a traitor." He was very angry. The colleagues who were at the table, were shocked. It was the cruellest surprise for me that I had never expected. It seems he did not like my critical talk of one of the Islamic groups that he supported. Luckily, he was not carrying a gun.

When I was in Algeria, almost daily I was put in a defensive position.

"What are you doing here. Go to Palestine and declare jihad on the Jews who have seized your land. Go carry a gun and kill them. This is how we Algerians defeated the French and kicked them out of Algeria. Go brother. Go back," was often said by some individuals.

This was daily talk from some shallow or narrow sighted young Algerians. Although I felt insulted, I managed to respond with confidence. "Listen, my brother. Jihad, which means struggle, can take different forms; and what I am doing in Algeria is a kind of struggle. I am working hard to get a university degree in English, and this endeavour, is one of the noblest forms of jihad or fighting according to our Prophet Muhammad," I explained. "You know, our Prophet said, 'Learning a nation's language is a shield against their evil'. In other words, it gives you access to their hearts and minds as Mandela said."

"I am learning English because it is a weapon to liberate my land from the occupier," I claimed.

"You know what? If the Israelis discover this fact, they will use their full power to stop Palestinians from learning English," I said. "English is more powerful than real weapons."

My coincidental encounter with the Canadian couple at the detention health centre at Algiers Airport in 1970 had shaped my perception of what jihad or a struggle is or should be. At that time, I was struggling desperately to convince them that we Palestinians were freedom fighters, as we used to call ourselves, and not terrorists as the media in the West had described us. The only weapon that was available to me at that time was not a Kalashnikov, but around 500 English words that I had accumulated after studying English for nine years at schools in Palestine and Jordan. To try and brainwash someone who is deeply convinced that you are a terrorist is a colossal task. Of course, you need more words. *From that day, I swore to acquire more English words and not bullets.* Sharif's words echoed in my ear. "The word is mightier than the sword."

I was only 20 years old when I had that encounter with the Canadian couple. That encounter generated a new conclusion, a new philosophy: Palestine will not be liberated by the Kalashnikov, but by the word. I took an oath to honour my father's principle that the pen is mightier than the sword. This new belief made me more determined to acquire the alternative weapon: English. English will be the pen that will challenge the sword. However, I knew that there would be a more challenging task, how could I convince those wielding Kalashnikovs to wield pens instead?

Three years after that encounter, I was still honouring that oath and using my pen to fight for freedom and justice. The main difference was that now I possessed thousands of English words, I also spoke at a good level of fluency and accuracy which captivated my audience. My audience were mainly my English teachers who came mostly from English speaking countries. I was delighted that my professors showed a great deal of interest in discussing the question of the Arab Israeli conflict. They opened their hearts and their minds and, of course, I had the ability to present my case adequately. I managed to be fair and avoid being too biased to the Palestinian side and that was necessary to get their attention and sympathy. Finally, I have put my English to service in my oppressed people's cause.

In those days, almost everyone I knew in the Palestinian community believed that force was the only way to liberate Palestine. I did not. I even suggested a federation between Israel and Palestine, something unthinkable in those days.

My teachers invited me to their houses for dinner and I spent the whole time talking politics. I really enjoyed those evenings as they did too. I had managed to answer questions, but I noticed that I did not have a very deep knowledge of history, religion, and international politics. "Why don't you recognise Israel? Israel claims that God had given them this land, what do you say? The Jews need a country, etc." I had a tough time dealing with all these questions and comments.

Chapter 12
The Cooperation Between My French and My English

It had never occurred to me that one day I would almost become a French citizen. The French chapter of my life is one of the nicest stories you can hear. By befriending French people in Algeria, I managed to secure myself a place in the heart of French society. Although it was the era of hijacking and Palestinians were seen as the main culprits by almost everyone in the West, I was well received by the French peasant society and was welcomed heartily. Those families had shunned the idea that they might be giving refuge to a terrorist and had complete trust in me. So, I finally found myself a home. I would never go back to Damascus because for my brothers whether I was in sight, or out of sight, I was out of their heart.

France became the place where I would spend my summer holidays. I lived with a family that considered me as a member of that family and they treated me as one of them. My mother Hamda's prayers came true. Before her death, she used to raise her hands to heavens while seated on her prayer mat and pray, "God send Ghassoub, son of Hamda, the most sympathetic people." And he did, first, the Official at the Embassy in Damascus, and now, these French peasants, who are one of the kindest, and the most sympathetic people in the world. They proved to the world around them that one must get to know others before judging them.

So, how did I succeed in entering France and settling with a French family to work in their farm in the summer at a point when Palestinians were seen as some of the most dangerous terrorists and hijackers in the world. The story started when one night, my roommate convinced me to write a letter to a French man who gave his address to him while visiting refugee camps in Jordan after the 1967 war. After exchanging a few letters, the French man, who was in his mid-60s, invited both of us to spend the summer holidays with him in Paris. We could not believe our luck.

While we were preparing to go to stay with that man in Paris, another French friend, who was working in Oran in Algeria, suggested we work in his Family's farm in Sothern France before going to Paris so we could make some money. We agreed on the spot as we had little money. We thanked our God for this coincidence that we had not expected at all. Can you imagine the risk that family had taken when they agreed to let us live among them despite the continued warning from others that they might be harbouring criminals? Even some went too far to say that they were planting a timed bomb in their own house. Truly, the whole universe was conspiring to help us achieve our dream to visit France.

As time went by and I settled with my French family in the breath-taking French countryside in Southern France, I was able to know their neighbours, their associates, their close and extended family members, and they introduced me to everyone they knew. They even took me to syndicate meetings as they were educated peasant activists. Besides, while working on the farm, I met many young men and women who converged on the region from all over France to work and make some money during the summer break.

Due to my sociability, French people's talkativeness and friendliness, and my aptitude, all these factors created an ideal environment for my French to improve. My French progressed at a lightning speed. And as a result, I was able to talk politics to a large extent by the end of the first two weeks. Thanks to the excellent French consulate's course in Algiers two years before that had laid strong foundations which enabled me to pick up language so easily and quickly. I was even acquiring a nice accent. I spoke accurately, fluently, and just paused sometimes to find a word, and if this failed, I went round it and managed to convey the message to my interlocutors.

I began to act like an ambassador of Palestine in that region. People's curiosity whenever they heard the word Palestine, motivated me to talk. So, Palestine became the main topic of any conversation. Peasants, friends of my friends, extended family members began to invite me for dinners and picnics so I could talk about Palestine.

Now, my French language in my brain's left hemisphere began to push English aside and let it sleep while I was in France. I rarely spoke English because in France 'we speak French only'. This deeply held tradition helped me perfect my French. But my desire and my desperate attempt to present the Palestinian people's just cause had helped me to learn French.

By the end of my six weeks in that region, I had managed to clarify some of the ambiguity that had surrounded the Palestinian people in European minds. People began to distinguish between the victim and the persecutor. More importantly, they would not generalise the misperception of terrorism to the whole Palestinian nation because those who committed the vicious air hijacking acts were individuals who did not represent the Palestinian people's aspirations and ambitions.

However, my biggest achievement in France was the friendship and the strong bonds that I had struck with the family that I lived with. When we were saying goodbye, they assured me that now I had a home in France that I can come to any time I wanted. This was 48 years ago, and this relationship is as strong as ever. *"Thank you, mother, for your prayer that has given birth to a new brother and sister in France."*

The biggest surprise took place was when I returned to Algeria and stood with my Algerian classmates in the corridor during break time. As they talked in French as usual and I was left out, this time, I suddenly joined in and spoke in my beautiful French, which made them pause, turn to me with dropping jaws. As the shock began to disappear and they recovered their voices, they all yelled, "Wow! Si (Si stands for Mr.) Mustafa. Now you speak real French." That signalled my integration in the Algerian society.

My message to everyone in this world is: "If you learn a language, you will uncover a hidden treasure." Unfortunately, many school systems around the world have maltreated languages in their systems by teaching them as school subjects. School students who interpret their success in every subject by the amount of grades they earn, have most of them missed that opportunity to learn languages and strike up friendships all over the world. Here is one last thing I want to say: "If you learn a language, you are contributing to spreading peace and minimising the risk of war in the world."

I'd like to share with you before ending this chapter a funny little anecdote about my first week in France. On my first day of work on the farm, I had to uproot asparagus. That was easy and even enjoyable; however, I had never heard or seen that before. But before I started to work, Jean-Pierre, my host, introduced me to his parents who were in their 60s. They were friendly but the father sounded very funny. After a while, I felt thirsty because it was getting hot that day. I walked to the end of the field where the father was standing carrying a bottle.

"Bonjour!" I said.

"Bonjour!" he replied.

"I am thirsty. Can I have some water?" I said trying to be as polite as possible using 'vous' and not 'tu.'

"Sure. Here you are," he replied, and he handed me the bottle he was drinking from.

I looked at the bottle in my hand with a sheepish surprise on my face and said shyly, "This is not water."

"Why?" he asked in a serious tone.

"Because it looks red," I said.

"This is our water in France. This is how it looks." He tried to sound serious.

"Water in Palestine has no colour," I replied innocently.

"That is in Palestine. But not here in France."

At that point, we looked at each other and we both burst out laughing so loud it echoed around the field. That was one of my first humorous exchanges in France. In that region, almost everyone had a great sense of humour. That was why I enjoyed every minute of my stay there and learnt French quickly.

Chapter 13
Learn English and Know Your Enemy

"If you talk to a man in a language he understands, that goes to his head. If you talk to him in his own language, that goes to his heart." Nelson Mandela.

In my final year in the English Department, an incident took place one day that is worth narrating because it taught me a great lesson. Mr. Murray, British, and one of my favourite teachers was lecturing on the history of the English language. The amphitheatre was packed with more than a hundred students. The lecture was interesting, and it was felt everyone was enjoying it because Mr. Murray, a friendly and knowledgeable teacher, was presenting new information.

Suddenly, a confident loud voice from the back seats interrupted the lecture.

"Mr. Murray, Can I ask a question?"

"Of course, Alhadi. You can."

"Why are we learning English?"

Everyone was taken aback by that *shallow* question. Mr. Murray who knew Alhadi well, smiled bitterly, adjusted his posture, and seemed to be getting ready for the confrontation. One could hear the arrogance in Alhadi's tone of voice. Alhadi's English was perfect, and he was near native English speaker. Besides, he was rich, good looking and he even had a car. Very few students had cars and Alhadi by that era's standard was a millionaire or maybe a billionaire. I thought Alhadi had joined the English Club rather the English Department.

"For God's sake, that young man had everything. What did he want?" I was eating my heart out.

"First, English can be your source of a good income, and in your case, Alhadi, your good English will help you rise to be an important man in the Algerian education system. Besides, you will have deeper understanding of the British and American cultures." Murray gave more profound reasons for learning English.

"But I am not interested in those cultures."

"Then you can learn about other cultures through English; thousands of books are published in English in all fields of life."

There was silence and a tense pause.

"I think the real reason for teaching us English is that America and Britain are planning another invasion. You know that Britain and America gave Palestine to the Jews. You do not know what is coming next." Then Alhadi paused. "They are our enemies. Why should I study their language?" Alhadi said straightforwardly.

Everybody was stunned by Alhadi's directness and assertiveness.

Murray listened with that big dry smile on his face and, instead of turning hostile or defensive, he responded calmly and said something I will never forget.

"Then, Alhadi. Listen. Here is my answer: learn English to know your enemy."

Alhadi did not retaliate. I think Mr. Murray's answer dumbfounded him. Alhadi just walked out.

That was a powerful lesson to all of us. I was glad that Alhadi raised the Palestinian issue, but he attacked the wrong person. Why should Murray, or any ordinary British citizen, or any other citizen pay for their governments' foreign policies? Coincidentally, Muhammad, the Prophet of Islam said, "He who has learned a people's language, has evaded their evil." Now this saying is open to many interpretations but confirms Mr. Murray's saying.

I used to say to Palestinian fanatic friends to not overgeneralise like Alhadi and distinguish between ordinary citizens and governments. Some agreed but the majority would shun my comments with a gesture. "You just want to defend your western friends. They love Israel and hate us. This is the truth," one friend commented.

The history of the English language is connected to the history of all other spoken languages in the world. The history of languages is really fascinating especially when you dig deeper into details in how languages have evolved to be what they are today. After all, without a language, we would be just like animals; our only concern would be food and water.

The first written language or languages in history appeared in the Middle East. In this region known as the Middle East history started. Do you know what the Middle East is? It encompasses modern day Syria, Lebanon, Palestine, Jordan, Egypt, Iraq, Turkey, and Iran. In 3100 BC, that is five thousand years ago, ancient Egyptians developed a written language called hieroglyphs. This system consisted of images. For example, if you wanted to write bird, you had to draw a bird and so on.

However, the Sumerians, another nation that lived in the Middle East at that time, 3000 BC, developed a more sophisticated writing alphabet which consisted of symbols rather than images. That was the first writing system in history. These symbols were called Cuneiform, which meant wedge-shaped. The Sumerians had lived in nowadays Iraq, which was known as Mesopotamia, a Greek word which means the land between the two rivers, Euphrates, and Tigris.

The Sumerians and the other nations that followed, such as the Babylonians and the Assyrians used cuneiform as their official language. As they did not have paper, they recorded their business dealings and other transactions on wet clay tablets using a stylus made of reed. Then the tablets were kept in the sun or put in ovens to dry before they were stored. Many of these tablets could be seen in the British Museum and Baghdad Museum before the latter was looted.

The greatest revolution in written communication that shaped our present written languages was the 22 symbols that had been invented by the Phoenicians, a maritime trading nation that had existed between 1550-300 BCE and lived in what are nowadays Lebanon and Palestine in the Middle East. The Phoenicians, who traded actively around the Mediterranean, spread their alphabet to many nations. The new alphabet's revolutionary innovation was its phonetic nature, in which one sound was represented by one symbol, which meant there were only a few dozen symbols to learn. This innovation had made the other two scripts, the Egyptian hieroglyphs, and the Sumerian Cuneiform, that had coexisted, outdated. That was due to the fact that the two scripts had employed many complex characters and required long professional training to achieve proficiency, which had restricted literacy to a small elite. On the other hand, the Phoenician alphabet symbols were easy to master and became accessible to anyone.

As the Phoenician system proved to be more successful than other systems in recording transactions, and as wealth and money were involved, the Greeks, who were engaged in active trading with the Phoenicians, were the first European nation to adopt the new advanced system. At the same time, many cultures around the Mediterranean adopted the Phoenician alphabet. This led to the creation of two ABJAD language families: the first is the Western family which included the Greek, the Early Latin, and the modern Roman; the second family is the Eastern family which included languages like Early Aramaic (Language used by Jesus Christ), Nabataean, Arabic, and other languages.

It must be noted that an ABJAD language is a language that uses ABCD etc. or aa, baa, taa as in Arabic. One important fact one must keep in mind is that the Greeks wrote from left to right while Eastern languages continued to write their ABJAD in the same direction; right to left. Of course, the English alphabet is a descendant of the Roman and Greek alphabet that had been adapted from the Phoenician alphabet.

English, which is spoken by more than two billion people around the world, is a relatively new language. All sources indicate that the history of the English language started with the migration of three Germanic tribes; the Saxons, the Jutes and the Angles, who crossed the North Sea from Demark and northern Germany, between 5-7 centuries AD. The native inhabitants of Britain at the time spoke a Celtic language. The invaders pushed most of the Celtic speakers toward regions now known as Ireland, Wales, and Scotland.

But how did English acquire this name? Most or all sources claim that the names English and England were derived from the name of the third tribe the 'Angles'. Angles came from 'Englaland' and their language was called 'Englisc' – from which the words 'England' and 'English' were derived.

Arabic has a somewhat similar story which took place between 1200-600 BCE. According to the Arabic encyclopaedia and most resources, Jurhum, an ancient tribe, immigrated from Yemen, in the southern Arabian Peninsula, after the fall of the Marib Dam. This tribe, which spoke Arabic, arrived in Mecca, nowadays Saudi Arabia. According to Quranic and biblical verses with some variations, Abraham, the father of prophets in Islam and the other two major religions, took his wife Hager and his son Ismaeel (Ishmael) to a place called Mecca and left them there. Jurhum, the aforementioned Arab tribe was migrating from Yemen toward the north when they found Hager and her son Ismail, (Ishmail) in a spot where a water well had just gushed out of the ground. Hager claimed ownership of the water and the tribe abided by that. The story tells that the tribe, Hager, and her son Ishmail lived there. The tribe taught Ishmail Arabic and he became the father of all Arabised Arabs. This is just one part of the history of the Arabic language.

One of the wonderful facts about English is that it has borrowed excessively from other languages. These borrowed words are called by *lexicographers* – specialists who assemble dictionaries – loanwords.

[13] According to dictionary. com "Loanwords make up 80% of English." What this means is that there is no such thing as pure English. English is a delectable, slow-cooked language of languages. As lexicographer Kory Stamper explains, "English has been borrowing words from other languages since its infancy." As many as 350 other languages are represented and their linguistic contributions actually make up about 80% of English!

Isn't that amazing? English has borrowed words from 350 languages! This must be entered into the Guinness world Book as English one of the world's largest word borrowers. The most influential languages in English are Latin then French whence English has borrowed most of the words. Arabic, my mother tongue, ranks as number 9 in the lending languages. For example, English borrowed words like algebra, alcohol, coffee, lemon, etc. But the biggest contribution that Arabic has offered to English, and world civilisations and languages is the Arabic numerals 1, 2, 3, etc. Can you imagine how life would be now without these numerals? Or imagine we are still using Latin numbers, and when we want to multiply 28 by 27, the formula in Latin will look like this: XXVIII X XXVII = That would be weird.

Just imagine that those lending languages, especially Latin and French, have filed a lawsuit against English to the International Court of Justice, accusing her of overborrowing, and even worse, borrowing without permission, and that is an accusation of stealing. If those languages demanded that their words be returned, English would go bankrupt. However, English is not vulnerable and will not stand such a trial in any court in the world. You know why? Because it is the language of the most powerful nation in the world – America. Besides, English is spoken by more than 20% of the world's population. In addition, it has become the most powerful global language. Therefore, no one can defeat the English language. Even English has become a threat to some languages in the world.

As a learner or teacher of English, you might be wondering about the reasons behind the fact that English has become a global language, and the most influential in the world. The first reason according to *speakenglishcenter.com*, is the vast British Empire. From 16-18 century, Britain had the largest empire in history. By 1913, this Empire ruled over 23% (412 million) of the world population, and covered more than 24% of the world's total area (around 35

---

[13] Which Words Did English Take From Other Languages? (2018)
https://www.dictionary.com/e/borrowed-words/

million km2). This definitely led to the spread of English over the five continents of the world.

As the Great British Empire crumpled, America rose after the second world War as the greatest military and economic power the world had ever seen. However, America did not invade the world militarily, rather its invasion took more effective forms. American business and trade were booming globally, besides, American technology, music, films, fast food and so on were becoming so popular that English was boosted to become an international lingua franca, (a language used by speakers of different languages) the language of entertainment, and the language of navigation, and whatever sphere you like to name.

As an English teacher, I notice that many learners try to speak with an American accent which is obvious in the way they try to pronounce the 'r'. This reflects the influence that the American cultural invasion has had on the world. In contrast, they find the British pronunciation of the 'r' very confusing and weird. They wonder why the British do not pronounce the 'r' in many cases, so 'park' is pronounced pahk/garden/gahden and so on. Imagine you are a secretary, and your British manager is dictating you a letter. It will start like this; *Dia Seh. We aah sorry to infom you that yua odah (Dear Sir. We are sorry to inform you that your order)*...Isn't that funny?

Those I have mentioned are some of the main reasons why English has become the most influential language in the world. However, I have reservations when sometimes someone claims that English has spread because it is an easy language. It is not an easy language. English is complex and, in many aspects, has no rules. It may start easy when you begin to say; *hi, hello, how are you*? etc. But once you go deeper you begin to face serious difficulties in most parts of the language such as word form, tenses, conditional types, sentence styles, and so on.

I have a very important international personality that attests to my claim that English is not an easy language. That person is Pope Benedict XVI (16th), who died in December 2022. In a movie that named *The Two Popes* (2019), Pope Francis said: *"Speaking English is exhausting;* Pope Benedict added: *Terrible language – so many exceptions to every rule."*

Another difficulty is the so called 'Homographs'. If you have not heard about them...they are words that are spelled the same, and even sometimes pronounced the same, but mean different things. For example, tear (to rip) and tear (as in crying), bass (a type of fish) and bass (a low sound), bat (a piece of sports equipment) and bat (an animal), bow (a type of knot) and bow (to incline), just to name a few.

One of the weirdest facts about English is that it has no official language authority or committee that regulates it. By contrast, Arabic, Spanish, and French are controlled by councils that have some important functions. For example, Arabic has a linguistic academy, located in Cairo, Egypt, which approves or disapproves of new words. In the case of English, between 600-1000 word are added to the various dictionaries every year. These new words are decided on by lexicographers or wordsmiths. A lexicographer or a wordsmith is an editor and author of a dictionary. However, who has authorised these wordsmiths to edit dictionaries or add new words? I have not found an answer.

[14] The Oxford English Dictionary (OED), is one of the ten top dictionaries of the English language. Under the title: *'Here's How the Oxford English Dictionary Chooses New Words',* here is what has been published on this site www.smithsonianmag.com:

> Four times a year, a group of wordsmiths at the Oxford English Dictionary survey the evolving landscape of the English language to see what new words they should incorporate into what's been considered the definitive dictionary. While people may have different opinions on what slang terms and new definitions should be included in the dictionary, there is a serious vetting process each word has to pass before being inscribed in the OED.

For example, one of the newest words to enter the English language is the Italian word *'sala',* which means a living room. Coincidentally, the word *sala* means the same in Arabic slang.

It is interesting to see what the English wordsmiths will decide on the many Arabic words that the Dubai government has entered into its different systems to replace English terms. For example, the word *'SALIK'*, which means *road is clear* in Arabic, is now used instead of *toll gate*. Another is the word 'MARHABA', which means *hello*, and is used to mean *fast track service* at Dubai Airport. We might see these words in the English Dictionary one day.

---

[14] 'Here's How the Oxford English Dictionary Chooses New Words,' here is what has been published on this site: www.smithsonianmag.com

Chapter 14
From I Know My ABC To Teaching ABC

After four years, the moment had come to be crowned holder of a BA in English. At the end of four hard years of sleepless nights and unending studying, I finally could celebrate my success. With no ceremony, no gown, no cap, no Chancellor handing you your certificate with a firm handshake and loud applause from the audience, instead a receptionist at the counter in the English Department handed me two pieces of paper and asked me to sign.

"Felicitation," he said. That was a very quiet ceremony. I thought to myself, *considering the agony and the suffering I had endured for four years, the President of the Republic should hand me this piece of paper.* Finally, now I can say, "From learning ABC to teaching ABC," with confidence. Have I achieved my dream? I will be waiting for an answer.

The two papers, one in French and the other in Arabic, the administrator handed me were totally different to my expectations. The contents mentioned that *Ghassoub Mustafa, that is me,* had earned a license to teach English. The word license is the same in both French and Arabic. Here, I felt safer because in Palestinian dialect, we refer to BA in any subject as 'Leesans', which is the corrupted form of license. So here I discovered for the first time that 'Leesans' came from French. This would prove that I had a Leesans in English. The most important thing for me was that people would be convinced that I was a holder of a leesans. That was great news. I must say I dislike the word permit because it sounds like a driving permit.

On the other hand, I felt disappointed at the fact that no single word in English was used on the certificate. I reasoned with myself, how would an employer who knows neither French nor Arabic understand this certificate? The other disappointment was that there was no reference to English literature. English literature was a big thing in the Middle East. I knew that there was no force in the universe able to convince my sceptical brothers that this was a university degree in English literature. When they look at that piece pf paper, I would expect them to say, "What is this? Did you write this certificate? Why is it written in Arabic? Where is that Leesans of English literature? This piece of paper is worthless."

Although I was excited about teaching, my first job, which lasted only a few months, was in translation. My job was with an American company that was building a huge gas complex in one of the coastal cities near Oran. After working with the company for a few months, rumours spread that the company had fallen into a dispute with the Algerian government for failing to keep its obligation in meeting deadlines and so on. This resulted in the company's departure from Algeria. This cost me the loss of a good job, a good salary, and the loss of some good prospects.

One interesting thing that I kept in mind took place during my first interview with the chief American engineer of the departing company. After interviewing me for half an hour, and after I was given a written test by his assistant (an Algerian young man), I was called back into his office.

"You have done well in both the interview and the (written) test. You can start tomorrow. Goodbye," the chief engineer said briefly and turned his attention to some papers on his desk. I rejoiced at the great news and at the ease with which I had obtained the job.

I was carrying a Samsonite leather briefcase which I had borrowed from a friend to impress.

As I was standing to leave, I summoned my courage and said, "Sir. Don't you want to look at my BA in English?"

He immediately replied, "In America we do not bother about certificates. We care about what you know and what you can do for us."

Four years of pain and tears and nobody bothers to look at your certificate, I thought.

I said nothing. I just picked up my borrowed Samsonite and left.

My first job as an English teacher was in a secondary school (a French system lycée) in a small town in southern Oran not far from the Moroccan border. It was a huge school as it catered for the town and for all the neighbouring villages. As most topics were taught in French, the vast majority of teachers were French nationals. My excellent French gave me the opportunity to communicate with them and to befriend some. My knowledge of French was the talk of the town especially among other Arab teachers from the Levant and Iraq whose knowledge of French did not exceed some vocabulary.

I spent almost three years in that school. Being a mixed gender school, it gave me the opportunity of seeing how males and females acquired English and how they reacted to different strategies. My experience at school proved to me that Arabs of North Africa, especially in Algeria, were more prepared to learn English than their counterparts in the Levant because of their knowledge of French.

However, when it comes to comparing males and females, I came up with the unshaken conclusion and philosophised that girls are more willing to learn, and more disciplined in almost every aspect of the schooling process. In my three years at that school, I quarrelled with some rebellious boys, and on one or two occasions it developed into a fist fight which required the school security's intervention. In contrast, girls were always respectful, loyal, and peaceful. However, girls adore grades, and if they are not satisfied, they will protest.

In 1978 I bade goodbye to Algeria and arrived in the UAE to teach in the technical school system. When I arrived, the modern school system was in its early stages. Due to traditional customs, lack of motivation to learn and many other reasons, many children joined school late. Some students that I taught in the preparatory stage were my age, in their 20s. This made it extremely challenging to deal with certain individuals. They were undisciplined, very lazy, careless and they assumed that laws and regulations could be manipulated or compromised to serve their interests. These characteristics of students made teaching one of the most challenging jobs in the world in those days.

What worsened the situation was my tough character. To say the least, I was confrontational, bad tempered, uncompromising, and thus I was not qualified to teach that group of students, or devils, to use the right word. I was advised by older teachers to be as patient as I could if I wanted to survive. I was told to show more flexibility and treat these students differently because they were not like any other students. They came from a tribal background, and they were proud of their descent. However, they needed to be motivated to get some education as they still saw it as irrelevant and unimportant.

I absorbed that lesson very well. I began to adapt and survived in the school system for 12 years.

Those 12 years shaped my teaching and my educational philosophy. Gradually, I was transformed into one of the most patient and most flexible teachers in the world. I began to see things differently and came to believe that a teacher must be like a *chameleon* (a lizard that is able to change colour) so he/she could survive in every environment. The strategies and policies that I had employed in Algerian schools, for example, did not fit these students. Every situation is unique and as a successful educator, you need to develop the strategies that apply to each situation. I concluded, "If you want to teach devils, you have to possess the qualities of both devils and angels." My father used to say, "If you are too lenient, you will be squeezed. If you are too tough, you will be broken." So stay in the middle.

While teaching in school, I had the opportunity to have a part time job in a language institute in the evening. That was a completely different environment from school. The staff were all female native speakers of English and some, not all, were professional TEFL teachers. I was the first non-native speaker of English to join that institute. It seemed like a miracle that I managed to join the institute because most reputed institutes in Dubai and Sharjah would never employ a non-native speaker to teach English.

I worked in that institute for some years, then I had another chance to work in another institute at the invitation of its director. I worked in the same environment and excelled. Although I am not a native speaker of English, students loved my classes. As I developed a very good reputation, some requested to join my classes and refused to join any other class.

My non-native speaking teacher friends at schools were many and the news spread very quickly. For a non-native speaker to work with native speakers side by side was big news: many thought that would be impossible because institutes always rejected non-native speaking teachers.

"You have penetrated 'Troy's walls'. How did you do that?" one teacher asked sarcastically.

"You turned the tables upside down and defeated native speakers in their territories. This is an undisputed victory," another teacher said.

Have you heard of the *Tea-bags' Institute*? I am sure you have never heard of such an institute; besides, it would be unthinkable for an institute to be called this. It is true that I invented the name. The second language institute that I joined was located in Sharjah in a building on the first floor. On the ground floor, as in many other places at the time, there was a small Indian coffeeshop with two small tables and chairs on the pavement that sold tea in plastic cups. The pavement was bordered by a sandy area. That tea shop's customers would order a cup of tea, of course, served in a plastic cup with a Lipton teabag. They left the teabag to brew for a while, then they would dip it several times in the cup in a very automatic motion, squeeze it, finally tossing the teabag onto the sand near the table. Because the teabags were never collected or removed, the area ceased to be sandy and became a Lipton teabag field. That sight made me smile whenever I entered the building, whispering, *Teabag Institute*. When I joked with a colleague about the situation, she suggested sending a picture to the Lipton company as they might use it to promote Lipton tea.

Working in those institutes provided me with the opportunity to teach English as a means of communication to highly motivated students. In contrast, at school in the morning, I was teaching English as a subject to pass the exam to students who were rebellious and disinterested. And whenever I tried to deviate and teach them English differently, I failed. All they were interested in was grades.

Once, a mature student and may be the oldest in class, perhaps older than me and out of the blue asked loudly, "Mr., why are you ungenerous with grades?"

I said nothing because I did not know what to say to that shallow question.

"Grades are free, and you can give us as many grades as you want and that costs you nothing." Another one in the back said.

"Ya ya," everybody in class said.

I kept looking and said nothing.

"You are not paying any money from your pocket. So be generous and give us more marks," another said. This tells you how students and even the society saw the role of a teacher on those days; a grade dispenser.

Teaching in those two completely different environments at the same time, made me a seasoned teacher. In the morning, I faced a group of distracted and lazy learners, while in the evening I faced attentive and highly demanding learners in the real sense of the word. I felt like a European philosopher who had lived two generations: one before the [15]*Renaissance*, and another after. In both

---

[15] Renaissance is a period in European history that started in the 14th Century in which science, philosophy and other art subjects began to spread to replace ignorance that was widespread those days.

situations, I learnt how to manipulate every element to be victorious. In conclusion, working in those extremely different environments provided me with exceptional abilities and skills in the area of English language teaching and learning.

Chapter 15
Teaching Beyond ABC and How Do You Do

After spending 12 painful years in the school system and working in the mornings and in the evenings, I realised I had no time for myself nor for my children. Besides, I was aware of my unquestionable potential to teach English in higher education. I was urged by everyone I had met to apply to join a higher education institution. However, I saw that as a very remote possibility because my Teaching License would not impress any recruiting HR and my application would either end up in the waste basket or in a letter of apology wishing me better luck somewhere else. But that negative feeling did not make me abandon the idea of working in higher education entirely because I knew I was up to it. I still saw some hope and kept hanging onto a straw.

My chance of working in higher education came when the first college was opened in Dubai in the late '80s. Although my applications had been turned down in the course of two years, I had never given up, and I let my doggedness lead my resistance. As that college was run by a Canadian establishment, I had built some hope. I had the feeling that someone inside would act like that *American engineer* who gave me my first job as an interpreter based on my good performance in the interview and in the written test. He was very satisfied and did not bother to look at my so-called BA.

So, my determination paid off. And with help of an insider, I was finally invited for an interview. I did so very well in the interview that I turned the tables upside down and took the role of an interviewer for the last 20 minutes. The panel was so impressed that I was invited to a second interview with another panel within a week. In that second interview I presented myself as a seasoned teacher who was capable of teaching angels and demons and was offered a teaching position in a girls' college. I thought I had to take a second interview because I am a non-native speaker of English. That is just a guess.

In that college, I survived for 28 years working harder than anyone else. In that college, which was turned into a hive of activity by its dynamic director, I assumed the role of a working bee. I taught English and general studies to all levels, and I participated in all extracurricular activities. I even acted as an advisor for a business that was run by a group of students. The college became a centre of festivals and conferences, and I took a leading role in organising opening ceremonies and training students to be *Master of ceremonies (MCs)*. The ceremonies were organised so well that the director and everyone lavished me with praise.

One of my unprecedented initiatives in my college Golden Years was the creation of a speaking and reading club for students. This perhaps was the only initiative of its kind in all the 14 colleges that had operated under the system. My love for reading and speaking urged me to create that club, but the main driving force was the severe lack of reading among Arab students. The facts were shocking. In those days, it was revealed by research that an Arab reads six minutes a year, while, for example, an American reads 200 hours! An Arab reads two pages a year, while a British reads 11 books. That was dreadful but true. I do not think that the situation has changed much. Arabs, unfortunately, and contrary to their Golden Past, have very little or no passion for reading. The irony is the great Arab civilisation in the Middle Ages was unrivalled because it revolved around the book just as the planets revolve around the sun.

That Reading and Speaking Club (RSC) attracted many students who became campaigners for spreading the reading habit. They visited classrooms to talk about reading, they organised symposiums, seminars, conferences, and gave very interesting oral presentations to college students and visitors. Of course, all RSC's activities took place under my leadership and had been conducted in English.

Once, one British colleague sent me the following email after attending one of the RSC's seminars, he wrote, "*Your Reading Club was just amazing – you lit a torch for those students, and for other students to follow. Your students' presentations in the Reading Club were the best I've seen in the Higher Colleges of Technology (HCT)…intellectual, reflective, analytic…just great.*" That was a testimony that I had excelled in my job in and outside the classroom. I represented what the college director used to call 'an engaged core faculty'. This made me indispensable for the system and I served in that college for 28 years.

As I was beginning to feel that I needed a change in my teaching career as an English teacher that had covered more than three decades, I was offered to teach some history lessons, in English, to business students, besides my English workload. That offer was timely as it came at a point where I was feeling a little bit burnt out. I rejoiced at the news because I was so passionate about history and had been waiting for such an opportunity. Now, I was going to use English to teach something else. I felt that would be a great change from teaching the complicated passive voice, the hateful vowels, the impossible to understand conditional type 3, and so on, to teaching the Arab people's history.

However, teaching history to college students in the Arab World would be a great challenge. Those students had studied history at school and had a hard time with dates, names, and facts that they had to memorise for exams. I was sure this kind of curriculum must have made most of them hate history. Then, the challenge was compounded because the medium of instruction was English, and students would encounter so many difficult words.

I knew the rule of thumb; the first session in any course is the most crucial, and you either have students in your grip or lose them. The classroom can be your playground or your battlefield as McCourt said in his Book, Teacher Man. For this, I prepared a very interesting set of PowerPoints for the first session. The power points were animated and included very interesting videos, pieces of information, images, sayings by famous people, and quotes from Western historians that acknowledge the great Arab civilisation that dominated the world in the Middle Ages. This fact, which unfortunately almost all students ignored, made them curious. For example, the quote below made them gasp and look at each other, then look curiously at me as if saying, "Have you made this up? We know, we Muslims have done nothing." [16] I got one of them to read the quote below out loud.

"Muslim civilisation was the greatest in size and technology that the world had ever seen...the giant on whose shoulders the European Renaissance stood." Graham, P. 39

---

[16] Graham. M. (2006). How Islam created the Modern World. Pennsylvania. p. 39

"Wow, really? We thought we Muslims are just a band of terrorists." Students said.

My introduction to the course, 'The History of the Arab Peoples' went so well that in less than two hours I managed to transform most of those students from *'history haters to history lovers'*. This fact was acknowledged by them in the student's faculty evaluation at the end of the semester in which one said, "Before meeting Dr. Ghassoub, I hated history, and I believed that no power in the world could change my mind. But Dr. Ghassoub was able to make me love history from day one."

Once, I received an email from the Business Department Coordinator (BDC) in which he wrote, "A group of your history students passed by my office yesterday and they said that you have so fascinated them with your history information that now they arrive home almost half an hour late because they do not want to miss any minute of your exceptionally enjoyable history sessions."

I replied, "My friend, there is a secret in the word history; just drop the 'hi' and you will end up by the word 'story'. So, history to me is a story and I spare no efforts to teach it as a story."

When I met the Head of the Business Department at the end of the semester to discuss the annual appraisal which included student's faculty evaluation, she could not believe those comments. She thought I was a magician.

I commented, "Yes, you can say that. I entertained those students like a magician on stage. You know how interesting and gripping a magician can be? So, I do not mind if you say in your report: Dr. Ghassoub is a magician. I am sure this will be the right word for my annual appraisal."

Sha laughed and said, "Of course. Let's not forget your great sense of humour."

I taught history for more than 13 years and my students enjoyed every minute of the course. One of the secrets was that we got rid of one of the demons of teaching and learning, and do you know that demon? It is exams. I cannot forget the students' reaction when in the first session I announced that there would be no exams; they clapped, and some leapt to their feet clapping and shouting 'hurray'. That reminded me of our reaction to Professor Harry's announcement that there would be no exams in the TEFL course around 20 years earlier. History repeats itself. One of the great advantages of the history course was that it freed most students from the grade obsession. That was an unprecedent achievement.

In the history course, my students cared about the invaluable information they had gained and how this information influenced their life and their minds. Whenever they gave an oral presentation, for example, they cared about the message and not the grade.

They wanted the world to know that the Arabs and Muslims contributed highly to world civilisations between the eighth and thirteenth century AD. They led the world in medicine, technology, agriculture, science, arts and the list is endless. After all, it was the Middle East that gave the world the Arabic numerals: 0,1,2,3…[17]paper, and algebra and so on. Some students got so emotional to the point they were in tears while presenting these facts. What was remarkable was that they were not thinking about grades. They felt so awkward and so silly that they did not know these facts before because they wanted to prove to the whole word that Muslims and Arabs were not terrorists, but polymaths, scientists, inventors, and authors.

At the end of every history course, I told my students whom I considered my disciples:

"Now you have learnt your glorious history in the most important language in the world. Think of yourselves as ambassadors of your history, of your culture, and of your ancestors who gave this world the pen, the ink, and the paper. Above all, you have the noblest mission; you are ambassadors of peace and interfaith dialogue. Use your knowledge of history and your English skills to break cultural barriers, to understand and accept others, to make friends, and finally to talk to your enemies. Prove to the world that Islam is a religion of peace and tolerance."

My success in teaching history made me conclude that, *"If you are passionate about what you teach, your students are most likely to become passionate as well."* This is a formula for success. A teacher's passion is contagious.

I became so obsessed with history that I would dominate the conversation at lunch time with colleagues and direct it toward history. I began to send emails to interested colleagues to join me for a *history lunch*. Even the director himself

---

[17] Paper was invented by the Chinese but was kept a secret by Buddhist Monks until Arab armies defeated the Chinese in 752, at Talas River, and then spread the paper making technology to Europe and to the world. https://historyofyesterday.com/

was intrigued and joined my history lunch sometimes. With my story like style, my charisma, and my English, I captivated my audience at lunch who listened attentively and asked many questions.

In my talks, I touched on hot potatoes like sectarianism in Islam and the historical background to this hostility between the main two sects in Islam: the Shia and the Sunna. Another topic that I focused on was the history of how Islam spread and whether it was spread by the sword or by the word. I spoke with an open mind and tried my best to clarify all misperceptions. I noticed when you clarify misconceptions, *people feel relaxed and more secure especially if they come from another culture.* For example, when I explained the true meaning of the word 'jihad', which is misnamed as *'Holy War'* in English, the audience were astonished at the big gap between their previous distorted knowledge and what they had just learnt. To make myself more credible and less biased, I told my audience that my information about Islam came from western resources written in English which I had cross checked with Arabic resources. I explained the real meaning of *Jihad* to my misled audience.

Jihad means to struggle, to exert efforts, to strive, to take pains, to endeavour, especially in the sense of tirelessly, and to the utmost of one's ability. Jihad is an inner spiritual struggle and an outer physical struggle and to fight against the oppressor. Jihad, for example, is the struggle to build a good society, to overcome difficulties, or to campaign against something bad. Jihad does not mean to fight and spread Islam by force. The word Jihad has been abused by some fundamentalists and western media. The Prophet said, *"The best form of Jihad is a word of truth in the presence of an oppressive (unjust) [ruler]."*

Teaching and talking history were like a dream. I really enjoyed it so much as I could see the positive impact I had on my students and listeners. Knowing history means knowing the reasons why nations went to war against each other. So, when we learn history, we learn valuable lessons. Leaders like Saddam and Hitler did not learn from history, as a result, they plunged the whole world into death and destruction. If we do not know history or ignore it, we are bound to repeat mistakes.

Chapter 16
Why Arab Learners Suffer More While Learning English

The universal truth is that every language is unique and foreign language learners face certain problems while trying to learn another language. But the density and complexity of these problems varies from one situation to another. For example, a French individual will face fewer problems than an Arab while learning English. Having done a contrastive analysis of both English and Arabic myself, my research revealed that both languages have completely different structures, and they rarely agree.

So, how are they different? First, Arabic is a Semitic language that has a cursive form and is written from right to left. While an Arab has to spend time and efforts learning the English orthography (letter formation and spelling), a French person has already mastered that. Second, when Arab students get caught in the subtlety of the English vowels, they suffer from endless problems in spelling and in pronunciation. Another serious problem is learning and using the English tenses properly. English has more than 13 tenses which represents a massive task for Arab adult learners. I remember the frustration I felt whether to say 'I saw', or 'I have seen, or 'I had seen'…and so on.

Arabic is very flexible and tolerant when it comes to punctuation. One can write a whole page without a single punctuation mark and can use *'and'* before each item or action in a list freely. In contrast, English is extremely intolerant of any abuse or violation of its punctuation system. Arab learners, who find the system complex and not easy to learn, carry on writing English in an Arabic style hoping the teachers will sympathize with them and tolerate their mistakes.

I spent years working on my commas and full stops. And when I teach the system to my students, very few grasp the intricacy, but the majority carry on with their own style. What adds insult to injury is that when adult learners lack motivation and enthusiasm, they will find everything difficult and give up easily. This leads to the loss of hours and hours of teaching and enforcement.

Mastering the English tenses is the ultimate goal in learning this language because they are many, around 13, and are so complex. I had suffered during my early university years while trying to distinguish between for example, the present perfect and the past simple; between the past perfect and the past simple and so on. The most brutal of all was my failure to use the present perfect continuous or the present perfect simple. I spent hours and hours every day struggling with grammar books and dictionaries to know the rules. I called this the War of Tenses. Worse than that, mastering the rule does not guarantee correct use. What makes English tenses painful for Arab learners is that Arabic has only two tenses: past and present. Future is only a prefix or an inflection of the verb.

Here is one of my typical English sessions to demonstrate the problem:

"Did you <u>went</u> to the cinema yesterday?" the student asked her classmate in an open pair work activity.

"Sorry, you cannot say that. Although we understand the question perfectly well, grammatically, it is incorrect," I commented.

"You have to use the infinitive 'go' instead of the past form 'went,'" I explained.

"What is infinitive?" they asked.

After I explained, they protested, "But 'go' is the present form and the question is in the past. So, it's more logical to say, 'where did you 'went?'" they argued.

"That does not make sense. In Arabic, we just say: where you went yesterday? We need neither 'did' nor 'infinitive,'" they added.

I explained, "Logic is something and grammatical correctness is something else."

"This is a stupid rule," they said.

"No insults please," I said pretending to be serious. "Native speakers of English will not tolerate it."

They laughed. "Don't worry, sir. They will not take us to court. They cannot hear us."

"Maybe you are right. I have not heard of a court case where the plaintiff complains that his/her native tongue has been insulted."

Those humorous moments and the attack on the English language created a more cheerful atmosphere.

They were silent for a while. Then one asked, "What is plaintiff, sir?" And here we go, more explanation.

Once while I was having lunch in the college cafeteria with one of the Academic Heads, who happened to be Canadian, he asked about my day. He was very sympathetic, and I liked him. I complained that it was a heavy day because I had to explain a lot of grammar to students.

"I think my voice has gone rough," I complained.

Probably to keep the conversation alive, he asked, "What did you teach exactly?"

"The present perfect, present perfect continuous, and worst of all, the past perfect continuous," I said. As I knew I was talking to an educated native speaker of English, I thought he would sympathize with my trouble and understand this jargon.

Having heard that, he paused, stopped chewing, looked me straight in the face and asked plainly, "What is the present perfect, present perfect continuous…etc.? What are you talking about?"

There was a big childlike smile on his face, but you could say he blushed and felt embarrassed a little. I was astonished. An educated 50-year-old native speaker of English does not know the present perfect. He was amused by my astonishment and explained that he did not have to study any grammar as he picked up English from his mother and the environment. Then he enquired if this was applicable to Arabic as well.

That was an interesting discovery for me. Working in a multicultural environment is one of the greatest universities in the world. You learn something every day.

I told him, "Whether you are a native or a non-native speaker of Arabic, there is no way that you learn standard Arabic without learning its grammar."

This brings me to talk about the 'learning versus acquisition theory' in teaching and learning a language. One of the pioneers and leaders in this field was an American psycholinguist named [18]Stephen Krashen, who I studied profoundly while I was doing my master's degree in linguistics. He claims that "Language acquisition…is subconscious. We are generally not consciously aware of the rules of the languages we have acquired. Instead, we have a 'feel' for the correctness. While 'learning'…refers to conscious knowledge of a second

---

[18] Diesel. H. Stephen Krashen. Acquisition vs. learning. Krashen 1982:10
https://holgerdiessel.uni-jena.de/LA_Krashen.pdf

language, knowing the rules, being aware of them, and being able to talk about them." [Krashen 1982: 10]. This explains why sometimes many second language learners, especially adults, obtain high grades in grammar tests and fail to produce basic conversation.

The other language group that gives students trouble is the so called 'prepositions'. English prepositions are so many, and they are unpredictable. While struggling with prepositions myself, I was always confused about when to use 'on' 'in' 'at' etc. To help myself, I learnt some mnemonics. These little songs helped me in fixing my prepositions.

On for days,
From Saturdays to Fridays
In for months and years, for centuries
At for Easter and for Eeds, for times for correct deeds

One of the biggest difficulties English learners face in general in learning English, not just Arab learners, is that the spelling of many words is different from their pronunciation. This problem is compounded for Arabic speakers as their mother tongue has a Semitic alphabet and is written from right to left as mentioned earlier. Besides Arabic words are written as they are pronounced. [19]theconversation.com admits that English spelling is confusing and inexplicable. This fact does not require support because it is obvious to learners and teachers.

Just pay attention to the underlined words written in italics and their pronunciation between brackets in this poem used by teachers as *tongue twisters*:
Tongue Twister is a word, phrase, or sentence difficult to say because of a chain of similar sounds. (Merriam Webster Dictionary)

I take it you already *know (nou)*
of *tough* (tuf) and *bough* (baw) and *cough* (kof) and *dough (dou)*?
Others may stumble, but not you.
on *hiccough (hikup)*, *thorough (thorow)*, *slough* (slow) and *through* (throu)

---

[19] Why is English so hard to learn? (2016)
https://theconversation.com/why-is-english-so-hard-to-learn-53336

In this poem, each underlined word contains *'ough'* but each is pronounced differently! When I was going through this with a group of my students at university, they asked me to justify this chaos. And they wondered how they could master all that. I replied straightforwardly that I did not know exactly but speculated that these words might be loan words. The students looked at each other wondering how come the teacher, an authority on the language, did not know. I blamed the English language for putting me in such awkward and embarrassing situations. How could I justify this difficulty in English? I told the students to raise a complaint to the University Chancellor about the complexity of the English language. The session ended on a funny note.

Another *can of worms* – source of trouble – for all learners and Arab learners in particular, is the English verbs and noun forms. I tell my students to add 'er' to certain verbs to get nouns. Then they happily apply the rule, and they get 'singer' from 'sing', teacher' from 'teach' but when it comes to 'cook', they get shocked when I say you cannot apply this to your mother and say she is a good 'cooker'. Cooker is a completely different thing.

"This is unfair. My mother will be offended if I say to her 'you are a good cooker'. English is interfering in my life. Thank you for warning us, sir," they joked.

Sense of humour is contagious and if you have a good sense of humour, your students may catch it. I realised that making fun of the situation increases students' motivation to learn and to participate.

Then comes one of the most troublesome parts of the English language, the verb forms. We begin with the more friendly group, the regular verbs. As students add 'ed' to verbs in order to form the past simple, they feel relieved and thank the English language for finally showing some mercy on them. So, they can sail through verbs like pick, walk, talk and they feel relaxed.

But this sense of gratitude toward English does not last long as I, clumsily, mention that they have to remember the irregular verb group. I reluctantly say, "This group has no fixed rules, and the only solution is to memorise them. Or create your own mnemonics. So, *you do not sail, but in fact you* snail *in this group.*" They burst out laughing when I explained the word snail.

"How many are there?" one student asked. I hesitated and said, "Maybe a hundred," which was a lie. They shouted in disappointment and wondered how they could memorise such number. The voice in my head told me how they would react if they discovered that there are more than six hundred irregular verbs. So, my innocent lie was justified as it prevented a rebellion in the class.

Without doubt, one of the most tiring tasks in teaching English as a foreign language to Arab learners is correcting their essays and writing. Writing is like an endurance race. While riders have to cross, for example, 160 kilometres to cross the finish line, in writing a student has to write 160 words or 300 or more as specified by the task. In a controlled writing test, you can see them writing, stopping, gazing toward the horizon or at the paper, then resuming until they think they have reached the finish line. When students submit their papers, my endurance race begins. Teaching five classes a week with more than 20 students in each, this brings the total to more than 100 scripts that I have to correct almost every week.

As I carry my red pen, some of my students writing turns red. This is not the end of the story; you have to write comments and tell them how to improve. That is, you have to provide a study plan for each individual. In some cases, students need years and years to improve. Imagine the number of hours you put into this task. I remember correcting and marking papers while I was watching TV, while sitting with the family, and even sometimes while having picnics.

One of the most problematic aspects of learning English as a foreign language for many Arab learners is they depend on literal translation. Once they start writing they begin to translate their thoughts in their mother tongue Arabic into English. Just like when you want to transcribe some video content into words. Because Arabic and English are entirely different languages, their literal translation results in a very poor piece of writing. In some cases, the whole piece is written as one paragraph without a single punctuation mark nor any capitalisation. While correcting, I give up highlighting errors because it is endless. Sometimes, the whole essay must be rewritten. Can you imagine how stressful this can be when you have tens of essays waiting in the line?

So, how can we help Arab learners overcome all these difficulties and make learning English a smooth journey rather than a rough one?

We must encourage learners to read books in English. But for them to love reading, we need to help them find the right book. Once they start reading a book that they understand, they will keep reading and never drop out until they finish. One of the common complaints about reading in a foreign language by students is the fact that they abandoned reading books because they found them too difficult to understand.

Reading provides learners with endless benefits. First, it provides knowledge and information that will be stored in the mind as general knowledge or background knowledge. This knowledge will help them understand other books and other material. Second, reading provides learners with new vocabulary which will double their understanding. Thirdly, reading gives them a chance to learn writing styles and strategies. Reading is considered the main receptive skill that fuels the productive skills such as speaking and writing.

The second strategy to help Arab learners to overcome difficulties in learning is to encourage them to write in English daily. If they start a journal, and as they are writing regularly, they develop fluency and speed. As they are learning grammar and language mechanics like punctuation, they will begin to acquire more accuracy, and monitor their own learning independently.

Elbow, 1973 claims, "The most effective way I know to improve your writing is to do freewriting exercises regularly. At least three times a week. They are sometimes called 'automatic writing', 'babbling', or 'jabbering' exercises. The idea is simply to write for ten minutes (later on, perhaps fifteen or twenty). Don't stop for anything. Go quickly without rushing. Never stop to look back, to cross something out, to wonder how to spell something, to wonder what word or thought to use, or to think about what you are doing. If you can't think of a word or a spelling, just use a squiggle or else write 'I can't think what to say, I can't think what to say' as many times as you want; or repeat the last word you wrote over and over again; or anything else. The only requirement is that you never stop. (p. 12)"[20]

To improve writing, learners must be given feedback constantly and be guided in how to correct their errors by themselves. They may write several drafts until they end up with a correct draft. But through this process, learners become aware of their weaknesses and how to overcome them. If students, with the help of their teachers manage to create a Mistakes' Store of their own, they will gradually destroy those mistakes and errors. As a native speaker of Arabic, I discovered an interesting fact that errors in writing in English result mostly from interference from Modern Standard Arabic (MSA), whereas errors in oral speech come from colloquial structure.

---

[20] Elbow, P. (1973). Writing without teachers. New York: Oxford University Press

Teachers and students must be made aware of the negative interference of the Arabic language in learning and in producing discourse in English. This awareness will highlight the source of errors and provide strategies to avoid them.

For learners, they begin to construct better sentences and paragraphs, and their teachers advise them constantly to brainstorm and think in an English context. One of the successful strategies that I have employed as a teacher of English, is to get students to read a paragraph twice, hide it, then summarize it orally and in writing. Similarly, they would listen to a short dialogue or a monologue and summarize the content. Repetition will help learners to progress slowly but steadily. This process will help learners to move from dependence to independence and to take control of their own learning.

Chapter 17
The Hidden Battle for the English Classroom

Have you heard about this war? Native English-Speaking Teachers (NESTs) Versus Non-native English-Speaking Teachers (NNESTs). If you are not an English teacher, neither NEST nor NNEST, you probably have not heard about it. That is why when I joined the English Department at Oran University in early 1970s, I had never heard or thought about this hidden threat. However, the NESTs typically hold the upper hand in this war because they are more equipped and more prepared. They also think they own the English language.

I came to know about this cold war between NESTs and NNESTs in the early 80s while I was looking for a part time job as an English teacher in one of the private evening language institutes in Dubai and Sharjah, here in the United Arab Emirates (UAE). To my disappointment, almost all the ads in the English and Arabic newspapers about vacant English teacher positions mentioned clearly that the applicant must be a NEST. In some ads, it was mentioned not to call if you are a NNEST to avoid embarrassment.

I wondered why none of the professors at the English Department at Oran University, some of whom were NNESTs, had never cautioned us about that looming danger. They should have warned us about this possible war and prepared us for it. But perhaps they themselves had never heard about it. So, they cannot be blamed. Honestly, I felt as if I were living under an apartheid regime, and I wanted to revolt but I did not know how. This unfair rule had cost me the loss of many opportunities of getting a decent part time job, not to mention the feeling of inferiority that I had felt.

One morning in 1983 or around that date, I saw an ad in the English newspaper that attracted my attention. It mentioned that a well reputed institute needed a native English-speaking teacher, and to my resentment, that was written in bold capital letters. I thought this was a clear message to NNESTs not to call to avoid embarrassment. I felt deeply offended and very irritated. I cursed the circumstances that had led me to qualify in English. I regretted not taking my friends' advice back in Oran to qualify in law or philosophy or anything and to drop out English. "Now, when will this tug of war between me and the English language end?" I felt unsafe and insecure.

I decided to call that institute whatever the cost might be. I declared that the war had just started. "Not to be given a job because I am not British nor American nor New Zealander nor Australian is unfair and is considered an apartheid practice by the UN Charter," I justified my rebellion. Without delay, I went out to a nearby pay telephone, (mobiles did not exist at the time) and stood thinking and preparing myself for any unexpected shock. "What if the person on the other end turns out to be rude and rebukes me for wasting their time?" I shivered at the idea. Finally, I gathered my courage and dialled the number in the ad. I felt very nervous while the phone was ringing.

A voice on the other end said, "Al Kawkaba institute. Can I help you?"

"Hello. I am Ghassoub. Can I speak to the director?" I said in my somehow Queen's English. I thought if the director gets impressed by my English, he/she might accept to meet me.

"I am the director," came a male's voice at the other end. He spoke with an Arabic accent. *That was a good omen (sign),* I thought.

I immediately switched to Arabic because I guessed I was not talking to the right person. This was a clever move because I knew that the person to be convinced would be a Native English-Speaking person. I told him at once why I was calling, and I requested an interview. He was polite and spoke in a friendly manner.

He said firmly that they did not employ NNESTs and he was apologetic about that. I said I understood that very well but let the interviewer decide.

"I just need a 20-minute interview to prove myself," I said confidently. "I am not that typical NNEST. I am different," I added.

"We employed NNESTs in the past and the students did not like them. They had to leave, and we lost some business and reputation. Besides, it was embarrassing," he explained.

"Those schoolteachers had poor English," he complained. Then he paused. "Students insist on having a NEST when they join. Imagine the shock when they discover that their teacher is a NNEST."

"But I am not one of those teachers you are talking about," I said at once with an air of superiority.

After a little pause, he admitted, "True. You sound different. Where did you study English?"

I knew he would not be impressed. "Algeria," I said hesitantly.

"Algeria," he repeated. I noticed clear surprise in his voice.

"Well. I thought people study French in Algeria. But this is the first time I hear that English is taught there," he added.

After another little pause, I said at once, "But Arabic language and literature are taught in many western universities like Oxford and Sorbonne. So, what would prevent Algeria from teaching English?" I argued. "Besides, being in the English Department at Oran University is like you were living in England, or America." Immediately, I regretted saying that, but he made no comment.

"Really?" he asked. Then he gave a quick laugh.

At that point, I realised a positive change in his tone of voice. He sounded friendlier and less formal.

"Look," he said suddenly. "Although I am not very optimistic, I will present your case to my wife. She is the General Director and in charge of recruitment. She may agree to see you."

He paused. "She is British."

I understood the message.

"Okay then. Call back after one hour." He hung up.

The hour felt like a century. The worry I had was that if her husband could not persuade her to meet me, who else could? Then my case would be lost and no hope of a part time job. I comforted myself that the man on the phone seemed keen on me. This, I reasoned, might push him to put some pressure on his wife to accept to interview me.

An hour later, I picked the phone reluctantly and dialled the same number.

"If I am not offered this chance here in this respectable Institute, I will not have it anywhere else," I whispered to myself.

"Good news," the man at the other end said. "The Director has agreed to meet you. Come tomorrow at 5:00 in the afternoon."

I could not believe my ears. I was over the moon.

The second day I arrived at the Institute 20 minutes early. The man introduced himself as Murad with a firm handshake. He offered me a cup of tea and was very informal and friendly.

"You seem very confident," he said with a smile.

"Sure I am." I said, "Otherwise I would not have approached the whole thing at all."

At around 5:00, he accompanied me into his wife's office and introduced me to her, then closed the door and left.

To my great luck, the lady had a very clear and beautiful accent, something like what Dr. Phonetics used to call BBC English. She sounded, pure, clear and I did not miss a single word. Because I had a slight hearing problem and had some difficulty in distinguishing between certain sounds, I was extremely worried about that.

She touched on everything concerning teaching TEFL ranging from methodology, syllabus design, exams etc. Sometimes she would ask about something and let me talk uninterrupted for a few minutes. I knew she was testing my fluency, accuracy, and my ability to maintain a discourse. She listened with a smile all the time, which was a good omen, and I maintained eye contact with her. In fact, I had never ever spoken English with such confidence on that day in my whole life. I thought she was very impressed. I was determined to end the NESTs' control on teaching English.

At the end of the interview, after a little pause, she said, "Thank you," and I stood up and left. As I emerged from her office, I came straight upon Murad, who was standing at the reception. I looked at him with the biggest smile on my face.

"How did it go?" he asked. "Very well," I said confidently. "Go and check for yourself."

Without further hesitation, he disappeared into his wife's office. After a while, he reappeared and came straight to me and shook hands firmly.

"You did very well. She is so impressed. Well done." He shouted, "This is a historical day. A single NNEST has defeated the whole NESTs armies combined." At that point, we burst out laughing.

"Are you going to announce this victory in the newspaper?" I joked.

"Why not. It is an interesting story," he said laughing. "The headline would read something like that: A Single NNEST Wins the Battle." Obviously, Murad, who was a Palestinian, was very sympathetic to my cause.

He then took me around the Institute which was not very big and introduced me to some teachers who happened to be having a break. I felt amused that all the teachers were females, and above all, native English-speaking teachers. I knew that was going to be a big challenge to attract students to join my sessions.

In that institute, I made history. I built a great reputation and began to attract students. Even certain students would leave their NEST class and join mine. That was unprecedented. Murad used to wonder and say, "How do you do it? What makes these students love your classes?" Then he would add, "Now we have students who insist on joining your class only." In addition, the Institute changed its policy and began to accept qualified NNESTs to teach English. One of those NNESTs colleagues once joked, "Ghassoub, we must erect a statue for you as 'Ghassoub the English language liberator."

Then he added, "I am not joking. You have advocated equality in English language teaching."

Another commented, "The Nelson Mandela of English language teaching."

It seems the war with native speakers did not end. After a decade or so I came into another direct confrontation. This happened while I was teaching in higher education at a woman's college. The International English Language Testing System (IELTS), the most well-known system that tests individuals' proficiency in English and eligibility for higher education and for migration, was the issue this time. The colleges' high authority decided to introduce that system in the colleges and made it mandatory that every student must achieve [21]Band 6 in the IELTS Academic Module before graduation.

For one reason or another, it was decided that the oral part of the test should be conducted by NESTs only, and NNESTs can participate in administering the other parts of the test: Listening, Reading, and Writing. In other words, NNESTs are qualified for the robotic parts only! The NNESTs in the colleges, who were big in number, protested and wanted to meet with the management. I remember sitting in the Director's office discussing the issue with another English (Indian) teacher who said passionately trying to defend her case, "I dream in English." Then I asked at once, "Which English, British or American?"

The decision was cancelled and NNESTs were made equal to their NESTs in everything. This cancellation came after the Colleges directors in the country expressed their dismay at such decision. Many of them argued that NNESTs are

---

[21] A score of IELTS 6.0 or 6.5 shows that a person is 'competent,' meaning they can cope in a classroom situation even though there may be some mistakes or misunderstandings with language
https://ielts-academic.com/2012/06/28/how-to-get-a-band-6-score-in-academic-

effective and are highly professional in their jobs. They all had been recruited into their present positions because they were qualified to teach English at any level without regard to where they came from. The directors praised the NNESTs as some of the most dedicated and highly efficient teachers. In one email, a courageous director said, "Your nationality is not your Wasta." Wasta is an Arabic word that indicates '*influence, favouritism, or nepotism.*'

Regrettably, the hateful phenomenon still features in our daily life in many educational establishments, especially here in UAE. This discriminatory policy is still visible nowadays and deprives so many qualified NNESTs from work opportunities. I have done some research about the phenomenon on the internet and came across a quite big amount of literature on it.

[22] In a Blog, Arasi R. Wrote:

Hello Everyone,

I'm not a native English speaker but qualified to teach English. My entire education has been in English. English is the medium of communication I use at work and in my social environment. I have CELTA (Certificate of English Language Teaching to Adults) and yet almost all English teacher positions I have applied for are rejected on the grounds that I am not a native speaker. I understand some rationale behind this 'native only' request, but to imply that only native speakers are good at speaking or teaching the language is groundless.

[23] "Article 21 of EU basic rights reads as follows…Any discrimination based on any ground such as sex, race, colour, ethnic or social origin, genetic features, language, religion or belief, political or any other opinion, membership of a national minority, property, birth, disability, age, or sexual orientation shall be prohibited." https://teflequityadvocates.com

I believe, regardless of any consideration, any job applicant should be treated in the light of his/her qualifications and abilities and NNESTs are not exempt from the rule. If I had a language institute and I had just interviewed an applicant, I would not recruit him or her if they did not satisfy the criteria even if they were holding a PhD in English. Ethnicity will not be given any consideration at all.

---

[22] Blog. Created by Arasi R. 89 replies
https://www.seriousteachers.com/seriousforum1/356/hello_everyone_i_m_not_a_native_english_speaker_but_qualified_to_teach_engl

[23] Native speakers only job ads and EU law (214) How to tackle native speakerism and promote equality in ELT https://teflequityadvocates.com/2014/04/01/native-speakers-only-ads-and-eu-law/

If you are a NNEST, and you have never been into this mysterious war, or mysterious biased policy, in certain English language schools and institutes, you might accuse me of beating the war drums against NESTs and administrators. Let me explain…I found myself in this war in '80s because I had some ambitions. One, I wanted a challenging part time job because my full-time job was boring and did not give me any satisfaction. Two, I wanted to increase my meagre income in those days. However, until this day, many educational institutions put in their ads in the media that *'All our English teachers are qualified native speakers of English.'*

Chapter 18
You Can Sell Ice to An Ice-Seller

Once after giving an exciting presentation on the importance of reading at the Teaching of English to Speakers of other Languages – Arabia Chapter (TESOL Arabia) conference in Dubai in 2013, a lady from the audience came to me and said while smiling, "You can sell ice to an [24]Eskimo, or to an ice seller." Considering the content of the long and exciting presentation which focused mainly on strategies of how to convince stubborn students to read, I was so captivated by that statement that I decided to use it as the title of a future presentation. As it was long, I divided my presentation into two parts; the first part I called: *how you can sell ice to an Eskimo*, and the second part; *how to convince a horse to drink*. Both titles proved to be very attractive, unusual and my audience of English teachers got hooked and gave excellent feedback.

I am not sure whether I was born an accomplished public speaker, or it was my father's continuous training me to read aloud from my book, when I was nine years old, in the presence of his peers in our old home in Palestine four decades earlier, prepared me for public speaking.

The fact that I excelled in public speaking is still a mystery to me. But by watching old BBC videos, (we did not have the internet or YouTube those days) and by reading other stuff about public speaking, and by watching other speakers and learning from their strengths and weaknesses, I digested the secrets of successful public speaking really well. In addition, by training my students to present and to be Master of Ceremonies (MCs), I enhanced my oratory skills.

For almost 10 years, I had participated regularly in conferences and seminars as a presenter in the United Arab Emirates. Besides, I had been invited to present

---

[24] Eskimo: A person who lives in northern Canada, Alaska, Greenland, and eastern Siberia, the coldest environment in the world. Eskimos live on ice the whole year round.

at various higher education institutions in Dubai, Abu Dhabi and Sharjah. Most of the topics I presented had been relevant to teaching and learning of English. English language professionals who attended my talks, sent me emails thanking me for giving them very useful advice and recommendations on how to be more effective teachers. In addition, they congratulated me on my excellent presentation skills that made the sessions more exciting. This fact manifested itself in the rush toward me by the audience after each presentation. Some came to congratulate me, some to request my business card, some wanted the PowerPoints, some invited me to repeat the presentation at their institution, and some wanted my email etc., if you were an observer on that day, you would wonder about that celebrity surrounded by fans.

To attract students to read, I told teachers to give up the fallacy of giving English learners authentic material to read. This, in my view, makes students hate reading more because they do not understand what they have been given. I argued that if we want to get reluctant students to read, we need to provide them with texts that have been tailored for them, something they understand and a bit challenging at the same time. I also reminded that, for students to be able to interact with the reading material, they need background knowledge and vocabulary. As the rule goes, the more you read, the more vocabulary you acquire, and the more vocabulary you acquire, the higher level you go.

In one presentation at a TESOL Arabia Conference, I started by saying, "A proverb in Arabic says: you can lead a horse to the water, but you cannot force him to drink." The audience, mostly English teachers, nodded in agreement.

However, one farmer in America challenged this common belief and said, 'Yes you can.'

I paused and looked at the audience who seemed amused by the statement, but they were hooked.

"So, tell us how that farmer *forced or convinced* that unthirsty horse to drink?" someone from the audience asked.

You could feel the joyful atmosphere in the room which was packed: some were standing at the door and some sitting on the floor.

I said, "Easy. Just salt the horse and make him thirsty."

This was met by roaring laughter from the audience.

"Simple. Just add more salt to the horse food and make him thirsty," I added with a rising voice.

"So, what has this to do with reading?" someone asked. "Are you suggesting we can salt our students?" More laughter.

I loved that interaction between me and my audience; it made the session very lively and engaged everyone in the discussion. Just like my teaching sessions.

"Yes. I want you to salt your students to make them thirsty, so they want to read," I asserted.

Pause.

"So, how do you salt students?" I asked.

Silence.

That was a tough question because it was obvious that no one in the audience had heard of this Salting strategy before. You could see they were so eager to hear the answer.

"We offer them lemon drinks and double the amount of salt," someone said, which triggered more laughter.

At that point, I changed my slide and asked the audience to read the quote:

[25]*"Believe it or not, there is a way you can salt your communication that will make the other person terribly thirsty for what you are going to say...The more you want to raise the attention level, the more 'salt' you sprinkle into your words. This 'salt' is a statement, a group of statements, or a question that creates curiosity. When used correctly, it makes the person you are talking with...want to hear what we are about to say even more than you want to say it."* (Scott 1998.p.205).

After the quote was read and understood, I said to them, "I have salted you today by not answering your questions about salting immediately which doubled your curiosity to know."

They agreed and laughed. Then I gave examples of how I salted my students and activated their curiosity to read.

Once, I said to my students, "Do you want to know the secret of happiness?"

"Of course," they shouted.

---

[25] Steven.K. Scott. (1999) Simple Steps to Impossible Dreams: The 15 Power Secrets of the World's Most Successful People. Simon & Schuster

"Then, read this small book, THE ALCHEMIST." Of course, I provided a few details and how they can obtain the book.

This statement was very salty, and they pleaded with me to tell them the secret. I refused to tell them the secret or which page or anything. By doing this, I added more salt and made them thirstier.

I told them, "If you want to find that treasure, or the secret, read the book."

This led many of them to read the book and that increased their desire to read more.

I gave my audience more examples of how they can salt their students which they promised to try in their schools and universities.

After 9/11, I became active in presenting about Islam and Arabs' contribution to world civilisations. I presented the true image of Islam and demystified misperceptions about this religion. The audience, mostly western people and non-Muslims who suffered from Islamophobia, expressed their astonishment at the twisted information that had marred their knowledge in the past. With my strong background in history, I also displayed the Arabs' great achievements in their golden age from eighth to thirteenth century AD. I highlighted Arab contributions to world civilisations and to western civilisations in particular. Paper, Arabic numerals, Algebra, medicine, architecture, astronomy, hygiene, etiquette, an endless list of what Arabs and Muslims had contributed to the world. Without the Arabs, Europe would not be the same Europe now.

Finally, while reading this chapter you may have felt *salted* and you have become curious about that book 'The Alchemist' if you have not read it before. Besides, I may have salted you and aroused your curiosity about Muslim and Arab civilisation's contribution to world civilisation which I expect would motivate you to read about this topic. So, do not underestimate the power of salting.

Whether you are a teacher or not, you will need to learn the strategies of how to convince an ice-seller to buy your ice. My ability to salt had convinced many of my stubborn students to read which made them better students and more successful entrepreneurs in their life. I, myself, had been salted many times in my life which made me discover many secrets of success for my life and my career.

Chapter 19
The Best Teacher Is a Storyteller

'Once upon a time', or 'Let me tell you a story'. What happens when we hear that? We, human beings, once we hear such a statement, we suddenly drop everything, our ears pick up like watch dogs, our eyes turn to the direction where that voice came from, and we become attentive and ready to listen. It seems the human brain favours stories. No one can challenge this fact. The universal truth is that stories are more welcome than any other information in the human mind and they live longer.

[26]"The human mind seems exquisitely tuned to understand and remember stories – so much so that psychologists refer to stories as 'psychologically privileged', meaning that they are treated in memory differently from other types of material. I am going to suggest that organising a lesson plan like a story is an effective way to comprehend and understand." (Willingham. 2009, p.66) Thus, teachers should take advantage of how the brain treats stories to teach their students more efficiently.

To me, the human brain is like a landlord that owns two buildings, the left and the right hemisphere, and this landlord rents spaces according to the criterion whether the tenant is favoured or not. Stories are given a long-term lease and can reside and be active for as long as they want, while, for example, exam information that has been memorised, is given a very short-term lease, and is expelled almost immediately after it returns from the exam hall. If it resists or protests, the brain or as is called now – the landlord – will make sure this unwanted tenant is evacuated and dumped forever in the nothingness junkyard. Has this analogy explained the mystery of why humans love stories?

---

[26] Daniel T. Willingham, 'Why Don't Students Like School?' (Hoboken, 2009), 66

At home, when I was a child both my parents were storytellers. My mother was like a hypnotist: she told me bedtime stories to get me to sleep. I used to sleep with my parents and share their mattress. We all slept on the floor and that room served as a kitchen, a dining room, a bedroom, even a guest room. It was tiny and had only one little window, but it was warm in winter.

But the person who filled my life with all kinds of stories was my father. I think I was one of the most fortunate among my peers to have a father who was educated and passionate about knowledge and learning in that era of ignorance. Above all, he was one of the best story tellers in that era. My father's stories and tales were more exciting than those of my mother's as many were real.

My father had participated in the First and Second World Wars and he was a witness of those great events that shaped the world we live in now. He was a Sergeant in the Arab Army that fought the Israelis in 1948. In addition, he had a lot of stories about the Turks who ruled the Middle East until 1918.

Most of my father's stories were real, and they were so exciting that they gripped my whole attention. I was so thrilled that my jaw dropped, and my eyes were kept so wide open through the whole story that my mother at times laughed and said to my father, "Hey, old man. I am worried that you will charm this boy, and eventually you will transform him into a statue." That was true. My father had such a compelling style that he captivated his audience and had full control of their attention. I think I inherited the art of storytelling from my father.

Sometimes the stories were too long to be told at one go so he told me in instalments, just like Shahrazad and the king Shahryar in the Arabian Nights, stopping at a very exciting turn in the story. This was devastating to me because I wanted to know what happened. "Dad. Please tell me what happened. Did the hero kill the villain or not? Please carry on, Dad. Please tell me." Then I would turn to Mom who would be watching or busy doing something before bedtime, and would plead, "Mom. Tell Dad to continue."

Instead of asking him to carry on, to my shock, they would burst out laughing and Mom would clasp her hands and say, "God protect us. This boy is going crazy with your stories, Old Man." My father's face would go red with laughter, and he would turn to his diary to record what was happening at that moment in his journal.

Keeping a journal was something unheard of in that era and I guess my father was one of the few or the only one that used to practice that very academic habit.

Indeed, literate people in the village on those days could be counted on the fingers of one hand.

My pleas reached deaf ears – in fact my father was deaf, and screaming was necessary to get his attention – and I was not being taken seriously. So, I would scream, "If Dad does not tell me what happened, I WILL NOT sleep." There was no answer or any reaction to that threat. My mother who was bad tempered because of her chronic illness, which I did not know, would say, "Do you see that wall?" I did not answer because I knew what she was going to say. So, I would go to bed reluctantly thinking to myself why my parents don't take me seriously and let me know the end of the story. What would I tell my friends tomorrow who would be waiting to hear the story?

What made my father's stories exciting was not just the interesting content, but his style of storytelling. As the saying goes, "It is not what you say, it is how you say it." When I think about that now, my father those days used to employ his body language very efficiently to create an impact on his audience though he had never been trained in public speaking. His stories reached a climax when he used his *Rababa*, the Arabic ancient version of a modern violin. It is indeed the direct ancestor of the violin. It is made of strings and simple material but produces some strange music, however, it was popular. Living my childhood in that environment made me a strong believer in the power of stories, and above all, taught me the art of storytelling at an early age.

After 50 years, I discovered the power of stories in teaching. Although I had attended tens of professional development workshops and conferences on how to be an effective English teacher, no one had ever mentioned the power of a story in teaching. Teachers are very concerned with covering the syllabus, teaching for the exam, ensuring students are not complaining and staying safe. Ideas like students' enjoyment and engagement in the session are shrugged off by many teachers. Or these concepts are hard to achieve.

Being a humanistic teacher, I have always sympathized with my students and put myself in their shoes and imagined how humans suffer in a boring lesson. I wanted my students to enjoy my lessons and be engaged. For this aim, I have always searched for strategies and materials.

One evening while teaching a tough course called Business Ethics to a group of female Arab college students, in English as the language of instruction, I realised the session was not moving in the right direction. Despite my desperate attempts to make the session somehow interesting, the girls were bored, and soon would fall asleep on their desks.

The students that night struggled on two main fronts; on one to understand the concepts, on the other to understand new vocabulary that was related to work ethics. I decided that I had failed to attract my students' attention and I was pumping air into a pierced balloon. It was 6:30 in the evening and the session was scheduled to finish at 8:00. The minutes felt like hours, and I wondered how I could refresh my students' attention. *Easy,* I thought, *tell them to sleep and wake them up at 8:00 to go home.* But what if some fall into deep sleep and they refuse to wake up?

Searching for a solution in my mind, suddenly, I remembered my father's great stories and the atmosphere he created in the house.

So, without any delay I said loudly, "Listen, girls! Hey! Are you listening to me?" and paused again for a long moment. That brought some attention and the girls felt I had an announcement to make, in the middle of that boring session! How strange!

As almost all were looking at me idly, I said enthusiastically, "Look. I am going to tell you a story."

I did not know what happened at that moment but that was the first time I said that in the classroom.

Hearing that, the students' eyes went wide open, and all eyes focused on me like reporters' cameras focusing on a celebrity. Now I felt that I had gained more control of the situation in the classroom. I felt like a snake charmer, or a puppet controller. Obviously, the word 'story' had an incredible effect on those sleepy students.

Then I dropped a bombshell, "The story is about the Man who Sold his Wife."

I said smiling cunningly trying to maximise the effect. It was a rare moment and I wanted to take advantage and have the horse under my control. Now, almost all shouted in unison, "What?" and all exchanged looks. "Sold his wife! That's unthinkable!" Some pounded their desks, and some burst out laughing. But you could see the shock on all faces.

"Is this a true story sir?"

"Yes," I lied. I knew Thomas Hardy's story, 'The Mayor of Casterbridge' was fiction.

Until that moment, they did not take me very seriously as they suspected I was just tricking them to get their attention. But now the situation had changed. The students were awake and mumbled to each other.

"I am serious. I am going to tell you about that man," I repeated enthusiastically.

"Alright," they shouted. "Go ahead. We are all ears now."

Hearing that, I shook my head.

"Well. In this case, let's have a deal. It is 7:00 now and I will teach for the test until 7:40. You know the test is coming and you need to be prepared. Then at 7:41, I promise to tell you that story until the end of the session." I paused to check the reaction on their faces. I noticed the expression on their faces were different from the other nights or an hour ago. They looked livelier, better, and projected more enthusiasm.

"Okay?" I asked. "Okay," they yelled back. So, we struck a deal!

Having said that, I carried on explaining and teaching business ethics for the coming exam. What I could not comprehend was the unprecedented enthusiasm that the students displayed as I was explaining the concept and words; they asked questions, took notes, and they seemed to enjoy the lesson. I moved around the room, shuttled between the screen in the front of the room and the back of the room disseminating information, checking understanding, and throwing questions here and there to ensure they were awake.

As the hands of the clock on the wall was creeping toward 7:40, I felt there was an unusual movement in the class. I noticed that the students were adjusting their seating positions, sitting upright as if the air stewardess had just announced to the passengers to fasten their seat belts for landing. As the clock hands hit 7:40, you could see them closing their laptops and putting papers and pencils away.

Now 24 students were all gazing at me urging me to pay them their debt. "So, sir. Where is the story?" All spoke in unison. "It is 7:40, Sir. Tell us about that crazy man who sold his wife." Voices came from here and there. "You promised. We listened to you attentively, took notes like good students and now we want our reward; the story please." Silence. "No delay," they warned.

Now I was going to tell these 24 Arab college female students, aged between 18-20, some of them married, a few divorced, the story of Thomas Hardy's novel *the Mayor of Caster Bridge*, a series of fictional events that took place in the middle of the 19th century in England. In those days life was primitive, and I needed to portray rural England in that era in a way that Arab students could grasp a completely different environment from the one they live in now. Almost all these girls drive the most stylish cars and live in luxury.

I thought that would be the first time in my teaching career that I would tell my students a 256 page story from the heart of English literature. This is exceptional. But how can I recount that novel in half an hour? I had no choice because I had promised them and there was no going back. However, my main worry was what if they find it boring? This would be very embarrassing and bring an early death to my new teaching strategy.

I cleared my voice and said, "Of course, ladies. You are going to hear perhaps the most exciting story in your whole life."

Just before launching into narrating the story, I stopped short as I remembered something serious that could thrust me into trouble, and I might end up in the director's office. *How did I put myself in this mess,* I thought? *How can I tell these devout Muslim students the scene where Michael Hanchard the protagonist gets drunk and sells his wife in a moment of rage?* According to unwritten rules in the college, teachers should in no circumstances indulge themselves in talking about alcohol, drunkenness, and any related vocabulary in the classroom. In the past, some teachers were sacked for breaking the rule, and even deported.

I shivered at those depressing thoughts of deportation and felt anxious. I began to blame myself for not having thought about that earlier. The irony is that every year I take part in the orientation program for new staff, and I lecture to them for more than two hours telling them about what they should do and shouldn't do in and outside the classroom. Being an educated Muslim with long experience in teaching and working with non-Muslims, I was considered a vital source of information for the college. I was always consulted on matters related to culturally sensitive issues. The American director himself attended all my workshops to learn and to give the message to staff that this was a very important workshop.

My role in that environment was expressed by a British colleague and a friend in an email that read, "…you were a constant touchstone for all things to do with Arabia, the people, the history, the culture, the conflicts, the religion, always objective and honest, and always so knowledgeable and informative."

I reflected that it is just a story and students will not feel offended. Besides, they love me, and they have great respect for me. In addition, I am a Muslim and when I mention something taboo it is because I am against it. In fact, in the story, drinking is portrayed as the main reason for selling the wife because when Hanchard wakes up from his deep sleep the following morning, he discovers that he had sold his wife when he was drunk. As a result, he made a promise not to drink alcohol for 21 years to come.

Having expelled all my fears and worries, I felt better and more confident that telling this story would have a great impact on my teaching methods. It was an innovation. But before telling the story, I pulled out my mobile and held it high and said loud, "Girls, I am broke, and I want to sell my mobile now to the one who gives me the highest price." This act was another 'attention getter that fascinated and puzzled the students and made them wonder why this teacher wants to sell his mobile. What did the mobile have to do with the story? But this was another hook. It was the only thing available to me to demonstrate the key word in the story, which is 'auction'.

Some students participated and offered prices, of course, joking about it. One said 100, another, 110, and so on until one gave me a good price and I said it is yours. I asked, what do we call this kind of transaction and they said it in Arabic, *Mazaad*, because none of them knew the word 'auction' or auctioneer. That was a gripping introduction.

The rule is, if you are a teacher or a storyteller or whatever, you must make sure that your audience or interlocutors understand everything you are saying so they can enjoy it and understand the message. Pre-teaching difficult vocabulary is a must.

Finally, I began narrating the long-awaited story to an already excited audience.

"Once upon a time, in England in the summer of 1850, a young couple left their village looking for an opportunity in another part of England," I began.

Then I presented a clear image of primitive rural life in England in mid-nineteenth century when horses, wagons, and walking were the only means of transportation. To clarify more, I compared that era with life in the UAE when camels, donkeys and dhows were the only means of transportation. I managed to create the image of a young couple walking alone on a dusty country road in a summer day. The man is carrying a basket with some tools, while the woman is carrying a one-month-old baby. Apart from that, the couple's only possessions in the world were the shabby clothes they wore.

I made the scene more dramatic when I mentioned the names of the main characters, Michael, Susan, and the baby Elizabeth Jane. I wanted the audience to identify with the characters and live their ordeal, which they did.

So, I continued telling the story in my deep voice aided by my excellent story telling ability that was sharpened by my father's continuous teaching and coaching in the old days, and by my charisma that I had inherited from him.

While telling the story, you could see the serious expression on the students' faces, and you could hear their gasps as the sad events developed into the most brutal transaction that humans dare to do. Michael the husband, in a moment of intoxication as he got drunk, lost his senses, and sold his wife and daughter for a small price in an auction like selling slaves in ancient times.

Pausing and keeping eye contact with students when reaching a climax in the story, created an incredible effect on them. The brutality of Michael selling his beautiful and faithful wife along with his baby daughter was very hard to perceive and the girls were so moved that one shouted "If he were my husband, I would kill him." Another said, "Oh, these men. Nothing can please them."

But, I noticed, one student in the back with tears streaming on her cheeks. Being females, the students felt deep sympathy for Susan, the victim, and deep hatred for Michael. I think they had imagined that this was happening to them. After all, I managed to move them and immerse them in the story.

Another fact that sharpened my story telling ability was that I had listened to an audio version of the story more than one time. The narrator was amazing. He managed to mimic every character in the story and that made listening to the story very exciting. Indeed, I learnt a lot from him and excited my students more in my turn.

For half an hour, I managed to tell a big part of the story. The students had never been so attentive. They listened with such a great curiosity that I felt if I had given a test on that story, they would do very well.

I noticed that the clock was indicating 8:00 and that was already ten minutes after the end of the session. None of the students had noticed the time or even paid attention to it. They were so engaged in the story that they forgot to go home.

"This is the end of the first part of the story. Now it is 8 o'clock and you need to go home," I said.

"Oh, please carry on. Tell us what happened to Susan and the baby. Tell us more, please. We do not want to go home," they said.

I laughed with triumph. The session had ended, and the students did not rush home. Actually, they were moving very slowly and reluctantly. They did not want to go home. Isn't that astonishing? These students have full time jobs, and they study in the evening. They are supposed to be exhausted at the end of the day. But today, telling a story has reversed the truth and they are not rushing home. This must enter the Guinness Book under the title 'the longest that a teacher can keep his students willingly after 8 o'clock in the evening.'

I felt great satisfaction that evening when students kept saying, "Good night, sir, and thank you so much for such an amazing story," as they were passing my desk on their way out of the room. It was 8:30. And I left thinking about what fate was hiding for me. How would the director react when parents complained about that instructor wasting their daughters time in telling them stories about that drunkard who had sold his wife? Besides, they would be protesting about how he could mention alcohol in the classroom. Anxiety took grip of me, and my negative imagination kept producing endless worries.

I have an anxious mind and I always imagine the worst when anxiety takes hold of me. I am a worrier and I let my anxiety create all kind of looming dangers. I feel as if I am creating defensive strategies. I have that 'what if…' syndrome. People like me, with unjustified excessive anxiety, suffer and make everybody around them suffer, because their imagination creates a dome out of a small seed as the Arabic proverb goes.

While driving home, I tried to calm my nerves when I reasoned with myself that the director, who is an open-minded educator, would congratulate me on such an innovation. He would tell me that I had succeeded in engaging the students in the session which is the goal of every teacher. He, on every occasion reminds teachers to engage students. Engagement was a big buzz word in our profession. In general staff meetings, faculty, and staff, are always asked to define 'engagement' and to present strategies of how to engage everyone in college life.

So, that evening I concluded that a story is powerful, and I am one of the very few teachers that had discovered this truth. I promised myself that I would adopt a story-like technique in my teaching methodology from then on. However, telling stories in class would depend on the outcome of that night.

The following day, I was neither summoned to the Director's Office nor was I called by the Student Affairs Department to enquire about the drunkard who had sold his wife and how that was related to work ethics and the business course syllabus. I felt relieved and began to relax and think deeply about how I would make story telling a motivator for students to attend classes.

I usually arrive in class at least 10 minutes early, a habit of strong time management that I had adopted in my work life and became one of the secrets of career success. Sometimes I find a few students are already there, but the majority come on time and, of course, certain students come late. But for the session that followed the story session, to my surprise, most students had already arrived earlier than usual. I smiled and I exchanged 'hi' and 'salaam aalaikum' (peace be upon you) with the students who displayed a high level of enthusiasm. I wondered if that was the first effect of the story.

When I began the session, some girls interrupted, "Sir, are you going to complete the story today?"

Another in the corner said, "I have been dreaming of Susan and Elizabeth Jane and what happened to them."

Another said, "I told the story to my siblings and some friends that I saw last night before going to bed." Then she giggled and yelled. "Sir, now they want to know what happened to Michael. So, now many people are waiting to listen to the story. You know what I mean."

This was followed by loud laughter.

If someone, a colleague, or the head of the department was observing the session at that time, he/she would conclude that was a gripping introduction that would set the stage for another exciting session. The students were very attentive and energetic. Bridging between the previous session and this session was done successfully.

I laughed heartily at their comments as I had never expected that a story would have such an impact on people. I know the Arabs' love for aural literature. It is unrivalled and that is proved in 'the Arabian nights' or the 'One Thousand and One Nights', as the book is called sometimes. If you have not heard about that book, it was published in the eighteenth century, and it is a collection of exciting tales. Those tales had been told by Shahrazad, the Vizier's daughter, to the king Shahryar, which delayed her execution for one thousand and one nights. The book was a best seller in Europe. It has also been made into a movie.

I promised the students to follow the same program as the previous session. They agreed and they paid very good attention to *work ethics* as they waited impatiently for the rest of the story at 7:30.

At 7:30 sharp, I continued telling Thomas Hardy's story 'The Mayor of Caster Bridge' under the shocking title that I had invented, 'The Man who Sold his Wife'. I was able to manipulate their feelings and reactions to the turning points in the story. The story is full of stunning moments. The students enjoyed every moment and lived the events as they unfolded. That night, I had the most engaged audience in my teaching history.

When I marked that group's exam that semester, to my surprise and my amusement, their results were higher than I expected. They did better than in previous exams. Even, they were higher than other groups in the department. This proved that the story had motivated those students to work harder and achieve better results. But the other positive change in students' behaviour was that their attendance after the story improved a lot.

In the years to follow, storytelling became a predominant feature of most of my classes. I was always ready with a short story, or a joke, or an anecdote that spiced my session and gave it a nice flavour. Sleepiness, or day dreaming had disappeared from my classes. My students and myself enjoyed being in the classroom and always looked forward to the next session, which is something not very common in academia. It is an established fact in teaching that students rarely look forward to any session unless it is extraordinary.

I took good advantage of 'The Man who Sold his Wife' in my teaching but I changed my technique. I divided the story into small episodes of 5-10 minutes each which I would tell at the end of the session or in the beginning. Students loved the story, and they never missed a session because they did not want to miss the story. In my attendance records, the letter 'A' (Absent) almost disappeared and was replaced by 'P' (Present).

The head of the department had noticed that and in one of the monthly meetings he thanked me and enquired about the secret. "Dr. Ghassoub! Attendance records in general are poor, but yours are excellent. Can you share the secret with us?" I explained my experience in storytelling and the unexpected results. Most colleagues rushed after the meeting to find an interesting story, and some came to me begging for the 'The Man who Sold his Wife.'

However, telling an episode with a climaxed end at the start of the session proved to be a problem because many students got too excited and insisted that I continue the story. As I hesitated and declined to do that, that situation in some cases, got loose and distracted the students from the main objective. So, the purpose was reversed; instead of being a gripper, it became a distractor.

Therefore, I kept the story for the last 10 minutes of the session. The students always left the class with an emotional 'goodbye sir' and with a smile and promised to be present the next session.

Another strategy I followed in telling a story was 'inserting it in the session' while teaching. For example, I would pause every 10 minutes while teaching something from the syllabus, then switch to the story and tell the students one event for a minute or so, then back on track to teaching the syllabus. I noticed that most students were captivated by that approach, and I could see how attentive they were. You could hear the drop of a needle on the floor, as we say in Arabic.

That was a real novel thing in teaching. I think that was unprecedented in the teaching literature as far as I know. But that was a two-edged sword as I learnt from students later. Some students managed to keep switching from syllabus to story successfully and absorbed the material well, while some lost track of the syllabus, fell into dreaming and kept thinking about the story. So, I abandoned that strategy and kept the story till the end of the session.

I became so obsessed with stories in the classroom that I decided to give a presentation on the topic in conferences and seminars to professionals in the field of teaching and learning English. I always wanted to share my innovation and successes with my colleagues and other specialists. In fact, it is one of the topics that is not given enough attention in teaching and learning, unfortunately. After I became a storyteller teacher, I renewed my energy and my love and passion for teaching. Just as Steven Covey explained in his 7th Habit, 'Sharpen the saw.'

What doubled my motivation about the story method in teaching English was a book that I came across. The book is titled *Why Don't Students Like School?* The title was captivating and indicated that it was the right choice for any teacher to read.

The book prompted me to write an article titled 'construct your lesson as a story' in an academic journal that I lost track of. In that article, I started by quoting Willingham that if you construct your lesson as a story, your session will be like a James Bond movie that starts with a chase which grips the viewers from the very beginning to the end. So, your students will be more than lazy spectators in your session, they are not just sitting in their seats and watching, they are participating in the chase and taking part in it.

After decades of teaching English and other general studies topics, I concluded that the Story Telling Method (STM) is top-notch (the best). I have the evidence because I have been able to test my hypothesis. So how did I test my hypothesis? Sometimes, I could not use the STM in certain classes for some compelling reasons such as, syllabus pressure, lack of time and so on. I realised that in the classes where I was using STM, the students showed great enthusiasm, learnt more, enjoyed the sessions thoroughly, and achieved better results and so on. In contrast, in the sections where I could not use STM, the students did not feel very enthusiastic, showed some boredom, learnt less, and had poor attendance.

Chapter 20
The 7 Habits of Highly Effective Teachers

Since I put my hand on Covey's book [27]'The 7 Habits of Highly Effective People', it became an obsession. The information in the book was so useful and interesting that I read the book several times. Not only that, but I was also listening to the book audio version in the gym, in the park, while walking, and while driving. I think I have listened to the audio book more than 10 times. In brief, it dominated my world. I admit that after having digested the book, I became a better husband, better father, better human being, and a better (English) teacher. Then I began to regurgitate the information like a camel. I almost memorised the book.

As the TESOL Arabia conference was approaching, I wrote a proposal to the Proposals Committee for a presentation under the title 'The 7 Habits of Highly Effective Teachers'. As I was a regular presenter at the annual conference, the proposal was accepted without any question.

Covey's book provided me with a great framework and an ideal structure of my presentation. Besides, my four decades of teaching English to Arab students enriched my experience and made me a speaker worth listening to.

Aristotle, the great Geek Philosopher, who lived in ancient Greece around 2400 years ago, identifies a habit as achieving excellence when he says, "Excellence is an art won by training and habituation. We are what we repeatedly do. Excellence, then, is not an act, but a habit." This justifies why Covey talks about habits. He states that for a habit to be effective, one must have three elements: *knowledge, desire, and skills*. In other words, one must possess the *what, the why, and the how to*.

---

[27] Covey, S. R. (1989). The Seven Habits of Highly Effective People. New York. Simon and Schuster

In addition, there must be a paradigm shift. A paradigm is how we see the world. Covey confirms that 'the problem is how we see the problem'. For example, you can achieve a paradigm shift to the 7 Habits by seeing yourself as not a product of the environment, but as a product of your choice. Another shift is to be responsive rather than reactive. In other words, see yourself as a doer rather than a victim.

So, how did I adapt Covey's 7 Habits of Highly Effective People to teaching? What are the 7 Habits of Highly Effective Teachers?

Here they are:

Habit 1: Be a proactive teacher,
Habit 2: Be a reflective practitioner,
Habit 3: Be a Researcher and a Doer,
Habit 4: Be a student-centred teacher,
Habit 5: Be a humanistic, humorous, storyteller teacher,
Habit 6: Be a collaborative teacher, and finally,
Habit 7: Be reflective. Effective Teachers keep Sharpening the Saw.

Habit 1: Be a Proactive Teacher.

Yes, be proactive and inquisitive. In this habit, as a teacher, you need to understand as many aspects of your client's (student's) life and environment as you can. In this sense, you are looking at stimulus and response. Then what are these stimuli (prompts) that require your wise response (action)? First, you need to understand your learners' psychology. For example, what can cause a cultural shock? How would your students react to your feedback? What can offend them? What are their anxieties? They may suffer deeply from exam anxiety, grade anxiety, and language anxiety. For example, they may hesitate to talk in class or in public because they make mistakes, and their peers would laugh at them. Language anxiety is a great obstacle to making progress in oral skills.

In Habit 1, as a language teacher of college students, for example, you need to know your learners' educational background: the subjects they study at school, the length of school system, how they study English as a second language and their proficiency by the time they graduate from school, and how their native language impacts the process of acquiring a second language and so on. For example, if you are teaching English to Arab learners, you will discover that Arabic and English go in parallel, and they rarely converge. They are two different languages, and Arabic has a negative impact on learning English. As a result, you will find out the source of many of your students' mistakes that you have been wondering about.

Another important aspect of your students' social behaviour is to know about their religion or belief system, and their culture. For example, Arabs are mostly Muslims and there is a certain etiquette that you have to respect to avoid falling in serious trouble. A teacher or a businessman must know that most Muslim women, for example, do not shake hands unless on their own initiative. In our daily life, many foreign individuals get embarrassed by their ignorance of others' traditions which can affect their business negatively.

Another example: imagine you are teaching English to a group of Muslim men and women and one day you want them to debate *arranged marriage or polygamy*. These topics in a Muslim society are not open to debate because they are stated in the Quran. So, if you open them up, you will face resistance and the matter may get more complicated. Coming from another culture, you may make comments on your students' dress code, their makeup, or their Henna (dye) that many women apply to hands for special occasions. The examples of stepping into mine fields while teaching or doing business in another culture are endless. So be a proactive teacher to achieve excellence.

Habit 2: Be a Reflective Practitioner.

Confucius, the great Chinese philosopher said, "By three methods we may learn wisdom: First, by reflection, which is noblest; second, by imitation, which is easiest; and third by experience, which is the bitterest."

By the same token, *Socrates* 470-399 BC, the great Greek philosopher said, "The unexamined life is not worth living."

From my experience, reflection is an essential practice in our life regardless of who we are or what we do. I became an expert on the subject because I did a lot of research on it while I was doing my doctorate, which led my mentor, Marion Williams from the University of Exeter, to declare me an authority on *reflection* in one of her keynote addresses at one of the conferences in Dubai.

Reflection is like a wheel; we reflect before the action, during the action, and after the action. In our daily struggle to make our teaching more effective, we face many dilemmas. We think about what to teach, how to teach and how to assess and so on. So, how do we take the right decision? The answer is by using intensive reflection before action. This enables us to design the right material and strategies for our sessions. Then we reflect during the action, that is, while teaching. If, for example, while delivering some material you find that students have great difficulty in digesting or they are getting bored, you must reflect very quickly and act. Or in other words, you need to change gear during the session.

For instance, my experience while teaching work ethics is a great example. Once I noticed the students' inability to cope and concentrate, I told them a story, and simplified the explanation. This saved the session and helped me to continue. So, reflection produces solutions.

By the same token, reflection after action is a very important tool in our daily life. It became my habit to reflect on every session I teach. I also introduced the one-minute paper that I heard about from our director. The one-minute paper allows students to reflect at the end of the session. You give them a chance to write feedback on the session anonymously: they can mention what they liked, disliked and if they have any suggestions. That proved to be a very effective practice and my students' reflection on my teaching became a very important tool to reflect on myself, on my methodology and so on. Besides, this increased my students' self-esteem and their objectivity. I treated my students as equals and respected their opinion. This is a trait that is not shared by every teacher. Certain teachers deliver the lesson and leave. Take it or leave it policy.

I also included peer reflection as another reflective tool. I kept my classroom door open and invited colleagues to my session from time to time and asked them to give me an honest evaluation of the session. My slogan is 'peer evaluation is a friendly critique of how to get better.'

Reflection, if practiced daily and seriously, will enable you to pinpoint what went well, what went wrong, and how to act. I advise every practitioner to adopt self-reflection, the student one-minute paper, peer evaluation, the supervisor's evaluation and not to miss any opportunity to get constructive feedback from anyone. Reflection is one of the best strategies to face the truth and put things right before it is too late. As the proverb goes, "A stitch in time saves nine."

Habit 3: Be a Researcher and a Doer.

In Covey's words, "*Seek first to understand, then to be understood*. (Covey's Habit 5). Research is a human and purposeful activity that aims at providing the practitioners with data that gives them the opportunity to reflect on their practices in their fields." So, research is connected to reflection.

To enable ourselves to acquire habit one, we must seek to understand our learners. The more research we do, the more effective reflective practitioners we become. Research reveals facts and that is the main requirement for critical thinking. The more you know about your learners' background, the more you understand them. For example, your students hate reading, lack motivation, do not meet deadlines, come late to class, suffer from stress, and lack time management. By knowing the underlying causes of these malpractices through your research, you will be able come up with solutions.

Be different, be a doer and be experimental.

Have you heard about the Jar of Life?

When I asked my students this question, they were amused and replied by asking funny questions, "You mean I can put my life in a jar, sir? How big is that jar? Is it made of clay or metal or glass? Or is it the story of the Genie and the Bottle in the Arabian Nights?" That question which students did not take seriously and made fun of led to one of the greatest experiments in their lives.

Some days later, I arrived in class carrying some plastic bags. The students were wondering and asked if I was going to give them a banquet in class. I said 'yes' and all roared laughing. Then when everybody had arrived, without any introduction, I spread a tablecloth and began to empty the bags' contents on the teacher's desk. Now, 25 college students are watching, with full attention, this weird act of their professor with a lot of expectations. The big surprise did not leave their faces and eyes kept wide open. What is this teacher doing?

After I had emptied all bags, I had a pile of some quite big stones, a heap of pebbles, a heap of sand, and a plastic jar on the teacher's desk. Now I began to explain the mystery to those astonished students.

I told them:

"The jar represents your life and your time.

"The stones represent the most important things in your life: religion, family, work, study, etc.…in other words, your priorities. The pebbles represent the less important things, but they matter." I gave examples, like going out with friends, watching favourite TV programs, etc.…

"The sand represents the least important things in your life." The students gave me a lot of examples like, washing your car, shopping for make-up, chatting on the phone, etc.…They are experts on those."

Then, I started the demonstration. I began to fill the jar with sand and pebbles until it was almost full. I ended up with barely two stones in the jar because the jar was full. The students realised that I had focused on the little things and forgotten my big things. That represented lack of time management and disorganisation. I forgot my big goals. I ended up frustrated and stressed because I had not achieved my priorities.

Then, I emptied the jar and began a new demonstration. I first put all the stones, which represented my big things, or my goals in my life, into the jar. Secondly, I began to put in some pebbles and sand. By the end, the jar stood containing all the stones and most of the pebbles and sand.

Next, I asked them if the jar was full, and they yelled 'yes.'

"No, it is not."

Then I shook the jar and managed to insert all the sand and the pebbles.

They all shouted, "Now the jar represents success. You have achieved all your goals." Then they gave me a big hand.

They concluded that if you manage your time, prioritise your tasks, be organised, deal properly with friends and family members, say 'no' sometimes, you will have a great jar of life. More importantly, you will have a stress-free life.

When they asked if I had invented this experiment, I told them that was not the case, that I came across the jar while reading and researching for information. They swore that was the most beneficial session in their whole life and I was their most favourite teacher. They claimed that other teachers worry mostly about covering the syllabus, giving exams, following rules and rarely does anyone teach them something useful in life. "You are the best teacher in the world."

In that class, where the attendance rate was very low and almost 50% came late to class, the figures after the jar of life demonstration changed dramatically. Late arrivals dropped to almost 5 or 0% and attendance jumped to 98%.

In their one-minute paper (which I normally administer after certain sessions), the students gave unmatched feedback. They loved the session and said it was the greatest session they had ever had. They realised that they had very poor time management and they had zero knowledge of the concept of prioritisation. They acknowledged that they spend hours in front of the mirrors applying make-up and end up missing deadlines and falling in trouble.

At the end of the semester, many said that the *jar of life* demonstration had changed their perceptions and made them more effective people at home, at work, and at college. They acknowledged that that session was an eye-opener and had changed their life for the better.

So my advice to my colleagues is to be an active researcher, a doer, and to teach learners what they need in life to achieve success and to not just focus on the syllabus. One last thing, diverge from the norms and show something different like the *jar of life*. This will make students love your session.

Habit 4: Be a Student-Centred Teacher.

This is an extremely important teaching habit. It can be summarised by the Chinese proverb that says, "If you give a man a fish, you feed him for a day – if you teach him to fish, you feed him for many days." In a student-centred mode, students are treated like partners who gradually become responsible for their own learning. And more importantly, students are at the centre of the learning-teaching process. In this mode, the teacher is aware of every student level, and he/she provides material and a variety of activities that cater for everyone in the group and not just for the elite in class. In other words, the teacher must follow an individualised learning plan that considers individual capabilities and differences. Teaching is not like working in a hot dog factory. This means that you treat all students in the same way and you ignore their differences. You must keep in mind that every learner is different from the other.

The teacher who possesses Habit 4, oversees his/her situation and is guiding learners to be in charge of themselves. The students gradually begin to control their resources and move from dependence to independence and to interdependence. Effective student-centred teachers enjoy a great relationship with their students which results in more trust and empathy. In contrast, self-centred teachers underestimate students' capabilities, and they end up teaching passive learners.

One morning, I received the following email from one of my ex-students:

Hello Doctor,

This morning, I read a quote and it reminded me of you. "You can teach a student a lesson for a day; but if you can teach him to learn by creating curiosity, he will continue the learning process as long as he lives." Clay P. Bedford.

You taught me in a way that no other teacher did and I am really proud to have a teacher like you. You are really missed this semester!

– Amna

Habit 5: Be a Humanistic, Humorous, Storyteller Teacher.

Humanistic teachers are on a continuous search for ways that strengthen their bonds with students. They are constantly reviewing their beliefs about students. Humanistic teachers perceive their students as partners that should be treated with respect. They always ask them for their opinions about the material, the activities, and the session. Humanistic teachers see their students as explorers that are trying to construct their knowledge. Humanistic teachers are humorous and story tellers. They miss no opportunity to tell jokes or stories to attract and entertain their students.

On the other hand, authoritarian teachers view their students as resisters, and thus they use force and compulsion. They see their students as receptacles to be filled with information, or raw material to be shaped. When I was doing research for my doctorate, I interviewed 28 English teachers at government schools. They all expressed negative views about their learners. They claimed students hate school and they do not want to learn. So, they had to use force to keep discipline and order. They also blamed the system that gave priority to exams and did not encourage innovation. So, authoritarian teachers blame the environment and the conditions.

As the authoritarian teachers see themselves as a product of their environment, humanistic teachers see themselves as in control of their situation. When I was teaching at a technical school, I faced one of the most challenging situations of my teaching career. Technical schools were seen by most teachers as dumping grounds for academic schools. As a result, they adopted tough and authoritarian strategies to be in control. Some teachers said to me, "Do not give these gangsters a chance, be tough." I did not listen to that. In my humanistic philosophy, I saw these students as victims of the system. They failed at academic schools because they wanted to do or study something else that was not available in the system, not because they were useless.

Perhaps they wanted to study art, music, or mechanics. For that reason, I did not adopt those negative beliefs about students in the technical school. I used methods that made them learn, enjoy the session, and prepared them for the exam as well. Of course, keeping discipline in class was very challenging, which required patience and diplomacy. To stay in charge, I put one foot in the humanistic field, and the other in the authoritarian domain. I acted according to the Arabic wisdom which says, "Do not be too soft so you can be squeezed, or too stiff, so you can be broken." In English it is simple: 'Be flexible but firm.'

"I would like to thank everyone for their hard work this academic year." This is how the technical school's principal always started his annual and only meeting. "The results of the public ministerial final exam are varied; some are good and some are not." Then he would pause. "But as every year, in English, the success rate is 100%. Well done, Mr. Ghassoub." I was the only English teacher at school. After loud applause, the other teachers would look toward me and yell, "How do you do it man? How do you manage these devils?"

Habit 6: Be a Collaborative Teacher.

In this habit, a teacher is cooperative and inspiring in every sense of the word. It is said, "A teacher takes a hand, opens a mind, and touches a heart." A collaborative teacher connects with everyone. On top of all, he/she is a highly effective communicator. He/she can see the big picture and know what everyone is doing in the field. One of the most important traits of a collaborative teacher is their ability to avoid conflicts either with students or staff. But whenever a conflict happens, they do not react, they respond and find a suitable solution and they create a win-win situation for all. I must explain the difference between reaction and response in this sense. When something happens, reaction is immediate and could be emotional and inconsiderate of the consequences, which can cause more damage and lead to regret. In contrast, response is more thoughtful and is not immediate, which leads to taking the right decision.

Collaborative teachers are open-minded, open to criticism, their classroom doors are open, and they are willing to share. They benefit from differences in other teachers. They welcome comments and they see their colleagues as critical friends. In fact, they are very cooperative, and they are givers. They contribute, they share, and they hide nothing. In brief, and as Covey said, Collaborative people believe 'that the whole is greater than the sum of its parts.'

Habit 7: Be Reflective. Effective Teachers keep Sharpening the Saw.

Abraham Lincoln, America's 16th President who led America in its biggest moral, cultural, and political crisis, said, "Give me six hours to drop down a tree, and I will spend the first four sharpening the axe."

In my 20th year in my previous job, and on the occasion of the renewal of my seventh contract, the college director asked me in a meeting, "How come you have not burnt out?" As all eyes turned toward me, I replied confidently, "I keep sharpening the saw." He nodded his head and was pleased with the answer.

Effective teachers who sharpen the saw are in a continuous process of self-renewal. They refresh themselves in the professional, physical, emotional, mental, social, and spiritual fields. Effective teachers are not exhausted or consumed by mistakes. On the contrary, in their mistakes they find powerful lessons. Effective teachers sharpen the saw by reading widely, by exercising regularly, by doing professional development, by self-retraining, and by expanding their social network. Those who sharpen the saw produce positive energy and stay positive in the worst situations. They also avoid the five emotional cancers: Criticising, Complaining, Comparing, Competing and Contending (challenging). (Stephen Covey). To describe these human habits as cancers is really admirable and I totally agree with Covey.

Without sharpening the saw, I would not have survived in the teaching profession for four decades. That is almost half a century.

I have presented 'The 7 Habits of Highly Effective Teachers' presentation several times at conferences and at some institutions in the United Arab Emirates. The audience that consisted of teachers from schools and higher education institutions raised their hats to me and commented that it was one of the best presentations they had ever attended. Some of them said that 'the 7 Habits of Highly Effective Teachers' deserve a book and not just a presentation. As one academic said, "Teachers are doing the most meaningful thing on earth, and they are struggling daily to persuade generations of learners to absorb some information that some humans have produced."

Chapter 21
My "English–Arabic Poetry"

Poetry is the place where human beings make their feelings and emotions public. I have loved poetry ever since I was a child when my father used to recite *ballads* (traditional songs) for his peers and guests in our modest house in the '50s and early '60s. A ballad is a folk song, written or spoken mostly in Arabic dialect. To make his recitation more exciting, he sometimes played his rababa. Rababa is the ancient Arabic version of a modern violin. It is indeed the direct ancestor of the violin. It is made of strings and simple material but produces some unusual music; however, it was popular in those times.

After entering school and having learnt to read and write, I came in touch with classical Arabic poetry as our curriculum was rich with old and modern poetry. By the age of nine, I became a classroom orator, the best at reciting poetry and reading aloud because of my father's continuous teaching and training and because of the charisma I have inherited from him. He used to make me memorise a poem and recite it aloud using my body language and all the possible oratory skills. He made me shout out loud, using eye contact and gestures, a special training that other children rarely had. I was privileged to have an educated father who loved writing, reading, and speaking. Above all, he had special fondness for poetry.

Every time he had a gathering of his friends in our modest house, he used to make me recite a poem or read aloud a text from my book for them. Those old men bestowed me with praise and admiration and predicted that I would have a great future in public speaking, as I have.

I loved free Arabic poetry, and when I grew older, I tried to write and imitate great poets like Mahmoud Darwish and Nizaar Qabani. But after mastering the English language and having read some works by great British poets, like Shakespeare, Chaucer, Wordsworth, and American poets like Emily Dickenson,

Wilt Whitman, T.S. Eliot, I appreciated the deeper, hidden meaning of English poetry.

However, I suffered on two fronts; one, the painful digging for deeper meaning that required an exhausting and exhaustive use of Arabic and English dictionaries, and the second, the boring reading of certain poems which lacked rhymes, had no internal music, and sounded like prose.

Arabic poetry is superior to English poetry, I think, and (I am expressing my opinion freely where no one has the right to object), because it is rhythmical and very musical. If anyone tries to write poetry in Arabic without rhymes, it will be dismissed, and their work will not be considered poetry even it has a deeper meaning. It is said that it was the Arabs, the Chinese and the Indians who introduced rhyme in poetry to the world. The Arabs are proud of their poetry heritage which made their literature one of the richest in the world. In the past, a poet was like a spokesperson for his tribe; besides, he circulated news just as social media channels do now, but the main difference was, he was a very trusted source.

The Power and Beauty of Arabic Poetry
There has never been a nation in history that valued and cherished poetry like the Arabs did. Poetry has never had an effect on a nation like it did on the Arab nation. A single sonnet of praise could raise an entire tribe to the highest level of glory, honour, and fame. Whereas a disparaging verse could throw it into the abyss of disgrace and shame. It had the power to ignite wars and to send armies to the battlefields. The poets were honoured and held in high esteem. The kings and caliphs used to lavish them with gifts and titles. Many of them had their own poets who chronicled their achievements.
https://www.fluentarabic.net/the-power-and-beauty-of-arabic-poetry/

My early attempts to write poetry in English started when I was teaching English in college. I wrote a few poems in a sarcastic style about my daily life and college students' late coming, frequent absence and lack of interest in leaning. My students enjoyed the humour in those poems which focused on their bad study habits and their lack of motivation to study. While I was reciting for them, they got so excited that it was hard to keep them under control as they laughed loudly and pounded on their desks. They said that I had a talent for poetry and encouraged me to write. They swore that no one had ever written about them like that.

But what made my *English poetry* interesting to the Arabic ear is that all the lines ended in the same rhyme with flowing internal music, and thus my English poetry had some *Arabic poetry* flavour. That was why when I introduced some authentic English poetry to my Arab students, it was met with no enthusiasm and was considered hypnotic: some pretended to sleep and snore. Unfortunately, my early poems have gone missing. However, if social media had existed in those days, those poems would have gone viral.

Now, my English poems that are included in this chapter revolve around two topics: peace and war, and the loss of my country; Palestine. The ability to write committed poetry in a global language like English, is a weapon that has been granted to me by my Adopted Mother, the English Language. But before doing so, she made me take an oath not to acquire any other Weapons of Mass Destruction (WMD). She also allowed me to write my *English poetry* with some *Arabic style* and flavour and justified that languages always borrow from each other.

I told my Adoptive Mother that I had already sworn a similar oath to my father decades before. I promised to be loyal to my father's Rule number 1 in life: "The pen is mightier than the sword." I reassured her (the English Language) of my sincere intention that I had written a poem to honour peace and my father's number one Commandment: *The pen is mightier than the sword.*

Poem 01

The Pen is Mightier than the Sword.

My pen is my sharp sword
And my sword is my sharp pen
My pen gained me the sympathy and love
of all women and men.

The sword bursts rivers of blood
Innocent children, women and men drown in red flood
But the pen penetrates our souls and hearts
It restores love, passion, and new life restarts.
My father, my tutor, and inspirer
Had preached me day and night

To never use a gun to fight
He reminded me: a pen, a wise word, a smile a day
He used to say,
"Bring love and keep war and disasters away."

For a world full of peace, I pray
And everyday
Is the International global love birthday
Take your pen, sign, and write
And swear in the name of your God
"To never carry a gun to fight."

Bury your hatchet and your gun
Invite your enemy, the past has gone
Let our children from every corner have fun.
let them play the game of peace and not war
On our tragic past, we have closed the door.
Let's dance and sing for peace and kindness
And turn our backs to the war and its madness.

Poem 02

A Birth Certificate

I wrote this poem in a moment of pain and anger when I realised that the world denies my existence and my belonging to my country. A Birth Certificate sounds like the strangest title for a poem because a birth certificate is usually issued by the health department and is simply a template where the official in the department fills in your name, date of birth and other details. This is a proof of the date and place of your birth. But in this poem, *A Birth Certificate*, my certificate had not been issued by humans but by *Mother Nature* and with all elements that participate in the event when you are born. There is neither a health department nor a template to fill in, but there are witnesses that have witnessed my birth. However, the main source of this certificate is my *Mother Country*, Palestine.

A Birth Certificate

I was born in the month of September
On a very scorching sunny day.
My father named me Alghadanfar
And then went back to collect hay.

I was born in a very ancient holy land
That land issued my birth testimony
The midwife and everyone agreed and signed
The sun and the birds took part in the ceremony.

I, the sacred Palestine, have clearly testified
That Alghadanfar was born here
To this I have signed. Nothing can be denied.
I will be his home, his land, his heart, forever.

Your tampered records are written in the sand
They will be blown by the wind
Alghadanfar's birth is engraved in every yard
Palestine is his homeland till the end.

Before the whole world, admit
This land, for millenniums called Palestine.
The Historical Court of Justice has given its verdict:
To change a country's name is heinous and malign.

Poem 03

I Long For
An Exile's Everyday Song

    I wrote this poem of nostalgia while reminiscing on my childhood and boyhood in my beloved country, Palestine. That childhood was a mixture of joy and misery, but it was the only time in my whole life that I had stayed on a place that I can call home, or country. Those beautiful memories of my childhood evoked many emotions which made my pen inscribe on paper and write this poem, which I called: *I long for – An Exile's Everyday Song*. The images of shepherds roaming the fields with their sheep, my father writing in his own diary with his reed pen, I am sitting under the old olive tree, my cat purring in my ear, and so on, all are beautiful images that are engraved in my memory.

I Long For
An Exile's Everyday Song

I long for…
Palestine, my ancestors' cradle,
The land of honey and milk.

I long for…
My father's sharp reed pen
Sliding on paper, thirsty for ink.

I long for…
The merry shepherds and their sheep,
Roaming the meadows and hills.

I long for…
My mother's most beautiful eyes,
The fascinating bluebells.

I long for…
A stolen home I am crying to see,
Under the sun that was taken from me.

I long for…
Sitting in the shade
Of the immortal olive tree.

I long for…
My cat's purr in my ear
On a winter's night.

I long for…
My father's stories told
Under the dancing light.

I long for…
The warm, salty, and
Uncompromising Dead Sea,
And the English lady saying,
"Oh, boy! Do you know the verb *to be*?"

I long for…
The days when I had a home
Like everyone else.
I long for…
The happy times before
I fell into the exile's abyss.

I long for…
The great times when
I had childhood dreams so profound,
When I always returned home
And I proved the world was round.

But when Palestine
Was ripped off the world's map,
I changed my view, and the world
Became flat, like a mousetrap.

I think the whole world is conspiring
Against this Palestinian, who is me.
Why does everyone want me to spend my whole life
Condemned as a refugee?

I have been deprived of my home, of my identity,
Of my rights. What is my crime?
I have been waiting for an answer
From the UN, from the US, from the EU, my whole lifetime.
Many innocent people have lost their lives.
And how many more will be killed? And still we
Have condemned ourselves to fight till the end.

This war will cease to exist
If we fill our hearts with justice, not just pretend.
Peace is engraved on my heart.

I have all my life been oppressed,
But I want my oppressor to be my friend.
Finally, Your Honour. If you listen to me,
I can state my profile, and my case to thee.
I have not killed anyone, nor invaded anyone's land
I've never usurped even a grain of sand.

Why have you ripped me out of my home country
And offered it to a gang on a golden tray? Be fair,
Admit your injustice, and end my calamity, or you
And history, will descend into decay.

Poem 04

The Day of Injustice

Yom Kippur is a Jewish religious holiday, when Jews try to make amends for their sins and achieve understanding with God. And to achieve this, they slaughter a goat (scapegoat) which is burdened with their sins. So, the goat, the innocent creature, suffers death to relieve the Jews of their sins. The other occasion the Israelis celebrate every year is what they call the Independence Day. But on this day, on which they created their state, they do not slaughter a goat because they have already slaughtered the Palestinian people. In this poem, which I call 'The Day of Injustice', I remind the Israelis, that what they call Independence Day is in fact is the day of the downfall of another innocent nation and the day of occupation and misery.

The Day of Injustice

Every year the Israelis celebrate 15 May.
They call it, their Independence Day.
Laugh out loud at what they say.
To me it is the Doomsday.
On which, God, they always betray.
On that day,
I became countryless and homeless
And have lived in decay.

Your so-called Independence Day
Is a day of military occupation,
Is the day of another nation's annihilation.
Your Independence Day is the day of prejudice
And is the day of International Injustice.

Confess!
The crimes you committed in 1948 on 15 May
On your independence and birthday.
You did evil and ran away.
You uprooted a nation out of their country,
You cancelled their names and their identity.

Laugh out loud at what they say.
They call it Independence.
Indeed:
It is the end of Palestinian existence.
History witnessed a bloody performance.
How did the civilized world show tolerance?

In the history of all mankind,
In every record, from East and West
It has been clearly testified
The holocaust was a crime of Hitlerians.
But why punish the innocent Palestinians
Who had to pay for crimes committed by Germans?
The Germans and the Palestinians
Are different nations,
They are neither cousins nor have any relations.
In two different worlds they have existed
But Palestinians paid a heavy price
for something they did not do
And their country, they had to sacrifice

In the end,
Let's forget and not pretend,
I extend my hand to conciliate.
I have cleansed my heart of revenge or hate.
Come! Come! Join me at the negotiating table
And let's end our tragedy of Cain and Abel.

Poem 05

A Visa to My Country

Can you imagine that you need a visa to enter your own country, issued by a foreign authority? How does it feel when you think about that? It must be nerve racking and cause deep feelings of rage and anger. You want the whole world to listen to your grievances and act. Here, poetry is a great platform to appeal for justice that has been missing. Despite the injustice that has been inflicted on me for centuries, I have not lost hope and continue to fight my oppressors with my pen.

A Visa to My Country

O my beloved captive Palestine,
My only shelter, my broken-hearted sacred shrine,
Do not weep; do not shed your tears for me.
Your deep heart is where I beg to be
Alas and alas, they, in the name of God,
Have usurped you and claimed, "This is not your land."
I am dumped in my diaspora. Why? I do not understand
They rattled the sword and warned,
"From entering this land, you are forever banned."
Why? In their holocaust, I had no hand.

In my diaspora, no one can endure my pain
It's as countless as the drops of pouring rain
The injustice, the denial, is driving me insane
Why? Why? I have not committed any crime!
Why have I been condemned as if I were Cain?
I am a simple shepherd roaming the hills
Cannot you hear the music of my sheep bells?
All I have is a cane, some songs in my head, and a flute
I and my sheep ramble on a peaceful route.

Every human being, with the sunset, returns home
Every worshipper returns to their dome
Every sparrow, every bird, returns to its nest
Even the sun goes east and then returns west
Every ant, every mouse, would die to return to its hole
Every creature, in its sacred home, buries its soul
Everything in this universe revolves; to its home it returns,
Except Palestinians, who have been exiled from birth
But Palestinians who have perished at least returned to the earth.
All my life, I have been standing, waiting at my country's bolted gate
I knock, I beg, I cry, I plead, "Why do I have to face this unfair fate?"
A voice roars, "Go away. You don't belong. Go get a visa."
What a mockery. Where is the UN? Where are human rights? All suffer amnesia
My gun will be my father's pen; my bomb will be my hoarse voice
My patience is abundance, my sympathizers are diverse,
And peace is my choice. Armed with my unmistakable right,
With my deep roots, with the truth, I will fight.

I pray for your icy mind to melt and your dark heart to lighten. Then,
Your eyes will be able to see the light. One day,
I will enter my country's gate without a visa
But with a universal welcome from Geneva.

Chapter 22
From a Miserable ABC Learner to an Author

Whenever I visited a bookshop or a public library in the past, I always dreamt of seeing my book on the shelves. I looked at those authors whose books were displayed at the entrance with envy and imagined my book standing next to them side by side. Believe it or not, I did achieve that dream as my book now stands on bookshelves in many bookshops and libraries around the world. **Additionally, it is displayed at more than 19 online links. Besides, my book has participated in some international book fairs here in UAE and around the world. More importantly, I have been invited to numerous book's signing sessions. This kind of event gives the person a great sense of achievement, and a dream has come true.**

So, what is the story of becoming an author?

When I completed my doctorate in 2003 and submitted my dissertation, my mentor, Marion Williams from Exeter University said something that triggered the writer in me. She said, "Now you can write books." When you hear such a statement from an author, who had written books, your self-confidence soars high because it is an acknowledgement that you can be a writer. Her book, *Psychology for language teachers*, had been one of the main texts that every language teacher doctoral student had to study. Besides, Marion was not easy to please and she always demanded higher standards in writing. So, when she said to me, "write books," I took it seriously because she meant, "you can write books." This, in fact, increased my self-esteem and made me believe in myself. It was like giving me a license to write in English.

Someone said, "Education begins the moment we see children as capable and wise beings." Similarly, one of my father's daily sayings was, "Teaching at a young age, is like carving in stone." When I wrote my first composition when I was nine years old, of course in Arabic, my mother tongue, my father, who was my mentor at that age, put all his energy into showing me how to write well. He kept correcting, changing, adding until he felt satisfied. But one thing my father used to do, he kept saying to me, "Boy, you are a good writer. I like what you have written. You have a good imagination."

"What is imagination?" I asked.

"It means, you can create things in your little head and develop a story," my father explained.

When my teacher saw my composition, he praised it and gave it an A. But the most rewarding thing was to let me read it aloud for my classmates who gave me warm applause. I think that rooted the writer and speaker in me. Thank you, my father.

When I started learning English at the English Department at Oran University, I used to struggle to construct a small paragraph. Writing in English seemed so difficult that I thought it was unlearnable. I attempted to construct meaningful sentences, but I simply did not know how. I tried hard to learn the basics; fixing my 'do', 'does', 'is' and 'was' and so on. I tried to figure out why we say, 'he has gone', and 'he went'. What's the difference? The vowels gave me such a hard time in spelling and pronunciation that I cursed them daily and prayed to God that they get an incurable disease and die. "Why is English such a complex language for God's sake?"

My conscience told me, "Stop it, boy. Stop blaming the English language, fool! All languages are complex."

So, writing and pronouncing, or even distinguishing between sit – set, bit – pit, hot-hut, became very difficult and extremely frustrating. They are called the minimal pairs and Dr. Phonetics did his best to teach us those, which I nicknamed the 'enemy pairs'. After decades of learning and teaching English, I still make mistakes in certain aspects of the language, especially, *the enemy pairs*. Anyway, 'to err is human.'

If you had heard me talking in English or had seen my writing in my early days at the English Department, some decades ago, you would have died laughing at the idea of me writing a book in English. How would a miserable beginner struggling with his verb *to be*, trying to distinguish between the use of '*a*', and '*an*' in front of nouns, trying to learn the effect of those so-called *vowels* on the spelling of words and so on, write a book in English? You would have concluded that the possibility of writing a publishable book by this miserable learner was zero. *Let him write a topic sentence first.*

So, how did I in a matter of some decades manage to transform from a miserable ABC learner into an author? And having my book displayed on international sites like Amazon next to well-known authors is something I cannot explain. Besides, my book found its way to book shops and libraries in the Middle East and in other parts of the world.

Writing a book is not an easy task. It is similar to starting any project, or to starting a business, or to starting a one-thousand-mile journey on foot. For you to minimise your risk and maximise your success in your business, you need to have some essential factors. For example, you need skills, a business plan, and capital. Similarly, writing a book requires certain factors. First, you need to have mastered the language, second, you must have the content and finally you need a plan.

In my early attempts to write a book, although I had the content and mastered the English language, I had something important missing, and you can guess what it was: planning was missing. As the wise saying states, 'If you fail to plan, you are planning to fail'. So, lack of planning slowed my progress in writing a book for some years.

However, one element was always available that fuelled my desire to write a book, and that was enthusiasm. Enthusiasm is the most important single factor that helps us achieve our goals and dreams. Basically, if you are enthusiastic and keen to do something, it means you are intrinsically motivated to achieve it, and nothing can weaken your determination.

There was something else that slowed my progress in writing a book—the fear of failure. The nightmare that kept haunting me was, *"What if...?"*

"What if publishers rejected my manuscript and no one wanted to publish it?"

"What if I ended up with a manuscript that was considered unpublishable and my dream of becoming an author evaporated?" My anxious mind kept repeating *"What if...what if?"* As I was trying to figure out the future, I imagined certain horrible scenarios and was very worried about something that had not happened yet. I was like someone making a mountain out of a molehill.

All these questions caused me deep anxiety and shook my self-confidence at times. However, my 'doggedness' that had saved me from failure before, triumphed again. Then I took an oath that I would win this tug of war with the

English language whatever the cost might be. There was no going back, and I was determined to write a book in English. There was no going back, and *I will burn all the bridges behind me.*

As I was so determined to write a book, but unsure of how to begin and where to start, I suddenly had an idea. I decided to write a small chapter about one crucial event in my past life to pilot and test my writing. When I was 15 years old, in the intermediate stage, I was caught smoking in the school premises by a teacher at the military boarding school. Unfortunately, and to my unfailing bad luck, that happened just one day after the school principal, with the military rank of a captain, had announced in the morning assembly, with the teaching and administrative staff present, in a clear and decisive voice that "Any student caught smoking in the school's grounds, will be *dismissed* from school on the spot. There is no flexibility or mercy. Do you understand?" All of us replied in unison and in a loud voice that echoed throughout the neighbourhood, "Yes, sir." That was like taking an oath to abide by the rule.

What a serious situation I had put myself in. The boarding school was my only shelter in the world, and I was, perhaps, the only one in 400 students that had no other choice. The only two shelters that I could take refuge in if I were dismissed from school were my country and my two brothers' houses, but both were under evil occupation, and I was banned from entering them. The former was under Israeli military occupation, and the latter was under my brothers' 'wives' occupation. I felt my chest compressed and my mouth dried as I began to think of homelessness. "Where would I go?" Besides, it was winter, and the weather was freezing.

I thought the events in that story were exciting and people would enjoy reading them. I called the chapter 'The curse of a cigarette', which turned out to be attractive, and I managed to write around 12 pages, which surprised me. Having finished that chapter, I gave it to some colleagues in the college to read and asked them to give me their honest feedback. As usual, only a few read it and gave me very good feedback. They said they had been impressed by my writing ability. They urged me to write. That was one of the biggest hurdles that I overcame toward achieving my dream. This step contributed highly to removing my [28]*writer's block.*

---

[28] A usually temporary psychological inability to begin or continue work on a piece of writing. https://www.thefreedictionary.com/writer%27s+block

So, if you want to write a book, try to pilot a sample of your writing before you begin. By the way, the full *Cigarette Story* is available in my book, 'Ashes of a Lost Country.'

One of the greatest activities of our daily life that assists us a great deal in becoming good writers is *reading*. It has been said by some scholars that, 'Books are one of the best universities in the world'. Contrary to common belief that the more we write, the better we become; in fact, and in my opinion, it is how much we read which determines how much progress we achieve in writing.

Unfortunately, some or many language teachers ignore this fact and mislead their students. So, they end up with students who are unable to write because they neither have the information nor the vocabulary for the topic. According to linguistic theory, reading is the main receptive skill while writing is a productive skill. So, for production to happen, we need raw material. Reading fills your head with knowledge, vocabulary, and information which are the main elements required for writing. Just like the production cycle. Being a book lover and a regular reader myself, I felt the production process was running smoothly in my head.

I spent years and years trying to explain this fact to my students at all levels to convince them to read.

> I used to say to them, "*Reading is the mother of knowledge and knowledge is mother of everything. The Arab World is facing a reading and knowledge crisis and the statistics in this field are shocking. For example, according to the statistics an Arab reads four pages of literature a year, while an American reads 11 books.*" *Most students used to laugh, and we moved on leaving reading behind.*

Reading continuously and enthusiastically provides the brain with nutrition that helps it grow well and become productive. Just like when [29]'food is broken down by the digestive system to give energy to every cell in the body. We need food to fuel our bodies for energy, growth and repair'. Similarly, we need 'Reading' to nourish the brain, so it grows and becomes a productive cell. Otherwise, it will stay weak and lazy and produce truly little.

---

[29] Digestive system explained.
https://www.betterhealth.vic.gov.au/health/conditionsandtreatments/digestive-system

This fact surfaced almost daily in my career as an English teacher when students, who never read anything, sat *staring* at an empty screen or *sucking* their pencils whenever I asked them to write something. "What's the problem," I asked.

"Sir, I have no ideas. I do not know what to write because I have no information." That was a typical answer. This stalemate was surely the result of that severe lack of reading and listening. If there were no raw material fed into the brain, there would be no production. You reap what you sow. If you sow nothing, you reap nothing.

One day, while I was suffering from writer's block, I noticed that I had not read about how to write a book. I thought I needed to listen to other writers' experience and advice. That was the right step in the right direction. So, by studying several books and by listening to some audio books as well on the subject, I accumulated a wealth of knowledge on how to write fiction and nonfiction.

Writing an outline, or a plan, or a mind map for your book was highly recommended by every writer or author. Planning before writing was emphasised in every book that I had read or audio book that had listened to. And that proved to be very true. Once I began to write an outline for my book, I was able to recall most of the events in my life, both major and minor. The great advantage of outlining before writing is it helps you brainstorm and recall most of the events, and most of the relevant ideas and information.

But the book that destroyed my writer's block and cleared the way for me to write was 'Angela's Ashes. A Memoir'. Once while I was chatting with an Irish colleague at work many years ago at his workstation, he suddenly said excitedly, "Ah! I know you love reading and I have a great book for you." He opened his drawer and gave me an English book, *Angela's Ashes,* by Frank McCourt. That was the first time I had heard of such a book or that writer.

The book was so exciting that I completed it in a few days. I returned to my Irish friend and said that was an amazing book and wondered how I had not come across it before. My friend laughed and said, "Although the book is a Pulitzer Prize-winning memoir, and a bestseller, it is not very popular in Ireland as McCourt presented a harsh image of Limerick, the city where he spent his miserable childhood, and many people felt offended."

Reading that book was a major turning point in my attempts to write a book. It was like a bulldozer that had cleared all the rocks that blocked my way. I fell in love with that book and McCourt's sarcastic style fascinated me and I decided to follow in his steps somehow. Besides, McCourt and I had a few things in common: we had mainly miserable childhoods and we both had mothers who suffered to raise a family.

The interesting coincidence is that McCourt and I ended up as English teachers after having done some other jobs. The most striking similarity in this aspect is that we both faced difficulties in getting jobs as English teachers because McCourt spoke English with an Irish brogue (accent), which made school principals in New York reject his application. Likewise, I was rejected by some schools and educational establishments in Dubai because of being a non-native speaker of English.

All these common things between McCourt and myself made him my favourite author. While reading his books, I sometimes felt that I had written those books. One of the facts that I had learnt as a reader is, "If you love an author and you read some of his/ her books, you will definitely get affected and you might adopt some of his/her style." That is true in my case. As I read McCourt's three books, and listened to them several times, I felt I am ready to write my book and it became a question of when should I begin? But when you teach, and as McCourt himself claims, your students fill your brain 24 hours a day, you have no free minute to do anything else.

One of the most exciting moments in my life was when I met Frank McCourt personally in March 2009 during the Emirates Airline Festival of Literature in Dubai. McCourt was invited to the college where I worked, and he talked to our students. I managed to have a quick conversation with him. When I told McCourt that he had inspired me to write a book about my mother and my miserable childhood in Palestine and asked if I could borrow the word ashes from his title 'Angela's Ashes', the author was amused and said that I could borrow anything I wanted. He wished me luck and that meeting was so thrilling because I had never imagined I would be meeting my favourite author. A month later, McCourt died. That was very sad.

Around eight years from that encounter with McCourt, I published my first book. I called it 'Hamda's Ashes'. Hamda is my mother's name, following the steps of McCourt and his book 'Angela's Ashes'. I could not believe it when I saw my book posted on Amazon and other sites, side by side with other famous authors.

Finally, I have realised my dream and have written a 370 page book. I and my family felt great euphoria and my children shouted proudly that their father is an author. They know many young people as friends and peers, but none has a father or a sibling who is an author.

When I opened my book for the first time and started to read here and there, the joy was indescribable.

"Wow. This paragraph sounds interesting. This anecdote is exciting. This little story is very funny. Did I write all that interesting stuff? Really? Where has this genius inside me been hiding all these years?" I continue leafing through my book and stop at a certain page or a certain paragraph and read something. But this time, this makes me raise my eyebrow in disapproval and I whisper, "Who's the idiot that has written this? It is you, sir." Then, I calm myself and say, "Don't be harsh on yourself. The readers may think differently."

Two years later, I broke the contract with the publisher as they failed to market my book in the Middle East and besides, they were completely online which meant my book did not reach bookshops anywhere in the world.

As I changed the publisher, I decided to give my book another title. I realised that the name 'Hamda' would not be understood by all readers. Apart from some Arab readers, many in the world will not understand and will keep them speculating about that name and this would cause the book to be ignored. So, I called the book 'Ashes of a Lost Country – The Tragedy and hope of a countryless Palestinian'. This made the book more attractive, and I have been invited to book signing sessions in several bookfairs around the country.

During the recent war between Hamas and Israel in Gaza, I advertised my book on Facebook as an essential reading for others to understand the background of this brutal military conflict that had been reoccurring regularly every five or six years. Many young people in the world have no clue about the Israeli Palestinian conflict, even here in the Arab world. Lack of reading and lack of curiosity have made many young people ignorant of basic facts about the world they live in. 'Ashes of a lost country' contains the story of this endless war between Palestinians and Israelis told by me, an eyewitness. Thus, reading this book will give the reader the necessary background to understand the news.

My book 'Ashes of a lost country…' tells the real story of how the Jews had been brought from their diaspora and settled in Palestine, AND, how the Palestinians had been evacuated by force and sent into diaspora. This process was described by the American Palestinian author, Edward Saeed, as 'pump in, pump out'. In addition, the book describes the history of Palestine and the Middle East focusing on the causes of this ongoing military conflict between Arabs and Jews.

As you read, you live the real story of a teenager who was sent into diaspora after his country had been invaded by the Israelis. This teenager, who also lost his parents and did not possess anything in the world apart from the clothes that covered his body, ended up facing the world alone from the age of 12. The boy's doggedness gives us lessons of how one can cope with hardships and turn failure into success. In a matter of some years, he transforms from being a poor boy to become a successful English teacher.

As McCourt says, "There should be a prize for those who rise from a miserable childhood to become teachers."

I keep repeating, 'writing a book is not easy'. I never imagined that I would be writing a book one day. However, my miserable childhood and my rough teenage years, and the turbulent history of the Middle East provided me with rich historical information to weave an exciting story. The paradox is *misery and suffering can be exploited to create an interesting book.* In conclusion, misery has one good side: it helps you write books.

Here, it is worth mentioning how authors had been treated in ancient times by people and high authorities in the Muslim Empire. Historians claim that the Caliphs (Rulers) of the Islamic empire in the Middle Ages, rewarded authors, and translators the weight of their manuscript's gold. Can you imagine the weight of books in those days? They were so heavy because they were written by hand on papyrus (ancient Egyptian paper), on rags, on leather and so on. Authors must have received a large amount of gold on those days.

In contrast, when I sent my book to a very important personality in the field of education, I did not receive even a small message acknowledging the receipt of the book. I wish I had lived in the Islamic golden age, not because I want gold, but because I want to be acknowledged and congratulated on this achievement.

However, one of the pleasing impacts of writing a book is that my students that I taught English felt so proud for being taught by a professor who is an author. This is something that does not happen very often. They have never even met an author in their whole life. Now, they can see an author daily or weekly. In Arab culture, authors are highly esteemed. Authors are admired because the ordinary person cannot imagine how one can write a book. Publishing books is regarded as an act that only extraordinary people can achieve.

My classroom's atmosphere has always been relaxing, different and characterised by storytelling. But now there is a distinctive advantage; it is more exciting because the teacher is an author who is offering his book as a reward for winners of competitions.

One of the several students who read the book wrote a long review and emailed it to me, but I quote the following lines.

[30]The words can't describe this masterpiece, it was a beautiful book, and the stories were very interesting. I sometimes felt intense sadness, shock, joy, and sadness in each chapter. I enjoyed reading the book; I learned a lot about history and gained new vocabulary…I carried the book with me all the time to read, whenever anyone will see (sic) the book they asked me about the content of the book, they were attracted by the cover. I proudly answered, "The author of the book is our doctor," and they felt so interested to read it.

You reap what you sow, or as Paulo Coelho kept repeating in his book 'The Alchemist', "When you want something, the whole universe conspires to help you achieve it." My apologies to Coelho; that is not always true because in many episodes of my previous life I was entirely abandoned by the universe that Coelho is talking about; it did not leave me alone but even conspired against me. However, I would give credit to Coelho that indeed the universe conspired to help me achieve my dream to write a book.

---

[30] An email from one of my ex-university students.

Epilogue

From a legendary learner to a legendary professor

If I hadn't majored in Teaching English as a Foreign Language (TEFL), my whole destiny would have changed. At that time, in the early '70s, the only choice available at Oran university for me was to choose an Arabic major, namely geography, philosophy, law or Arabic literature. If I had given in to my repeated failures in English in the first two years, I would have ended up in one of those majors and I would have studied something that I did not like. Then there would be neither a professor of English, nor an author. Besides, there would not be that warrior who would wage an *English language war* on the occupiers of his country. It is very difficult to speculate on my destiny if I had joined one of those majors.

But I handled my failures and took my defensive strategies from a nineteenth century renowned American inventor's story, *Thomas Edison*. You must have heard about him. Everyone in this world should read the wonderful story of Edison.

[31]"The famed American inventor rose to prominence in the late nineteenth century because of his successes, yes, but even he felt that these successes were the result of his many *failures*. He did not succeed in his work on one of his most famous inventions, the lightbulb, on his first try nor even on his hundred and first try. In fact, it took him more than 1,000 attempts to make the first incandescent bulb but, along the way, he learned quite a lot. As he himself said, '*I did not fail a thousand times but instead succeeded in finding a thousand ways it would not work*'. Thus, Edison demonstrated both in thought and action how instructive mistakes can be."

www.internationalstudent.com

---

[31] Where Did Thomas Edison Go to School? (2020)
https://www.reference.com/history/did-thomas-edison-school-5279b345f515e28.

My life has taught me that a mistake is a tremendous opportunity to know the secrets of success.

Thomas Edison was the most famous inventor in American history, though he spent only 12 weeks at school before he was dismissed because according to his teacher, Edison was distracted and unfit for school. In contrast, I and hundreds and thousands of children like me, spent 12 years at school, more than 500 weeks, and we invented *nothing*.

Oh! Sorry! I missed something here. To tell the truth, many of us invented new ways of cheating in the exams!

"Edison believed that instead of teaching students to memorise, they should be instructed to observe nature and learn the 'hands-on' way. Edison's perspective certainly worked for him, as he had 1,093 U.S. patents, more than anyone else in history." www.reference.com/

When Edison was dismissed from school, his mother, a former schoolteacher, took it on her shoulders to teach her son reading and writing at home. The humour in this story is that the expulsion of Edison from school gave birth *to the most famous inventor in the American history*. I just cannot help laughing! What a story! Nothing can be more inspiring!

"What do you mean?"

"I mean, if Adison had not been kicked out of school, perhaps he would not have invented anything."

"And he would have spent his whole life memorising books to prove he was worthy of school."

This reminds me of a little joke.

Once a physics teacher told grade 5 pupils to impress them, perhaps, "Isaac Newton was sitting under a tree when an apple fell on his head and he discovered gravity. Isn't that wonderful?"

A boy replied immediately, "Yes sir, that is very wonderful, but if Newton had been sitting in class looking at books like us now, he wouldn't have discovered anything."

Majoring in a powerful global language like English is different from majoring in other subjects like business, philosophy, economics and so on. By majoring in an academic subject like business, you become single minded, or as Abraham Maslow said, "Those with a hammer tend to think that everything is a nail." (Maslow, 1966) That means you have a limited audience, narrow scope and one purpose, that you want to succeed in this major.

But mastering a language helps you acquire a sharp sword that sends you to the *debating arena* to win talking battles and tough arguments. *Your sword is your word*. You will not be single minded, but you will be a global speaker and a global critical thinker.

In the '70s and since its establishment, Israel, the military force that conquered my country and left me homeless, or better say *countryless*, has been developing and acquiring the most sophisticated weapons of mass destruction, under the pretext of defending itself against me, *the poor miserable English learner*. So, believe it or not I was involved in an armament race with the powerful Israelis; they were arming themselves with fighter jets, canons, and so on, and I was arming myself with what? With the *English language* only. But, by means of this weapon, *the English language*, I penetrated the homes of some deep sympathizers with Israel who came from Britain, America, and other parts of the world. While Israel was firing live ammunition on Palestinian *stone throwers*, and demolishing their houses, I was retaliating against their hostilities by firing *words* from my *English Language Weapon*.

By majoring in English, I became self-sufficient, independent and I needed no help from others. English provided me with the weapon to defend myself and the tool to earn my living. I even developed my productive capabilities and provided help to others. After acquiring my *English Language Weapon*, I was able to provide a living for my poor stepmother and her two daughters living in the Occupied Territories.

In addition, English gave me access to endless resources that enabled me to discover the truth about the world and helped me ponder on the world's deception and misguidance. So, English has been nutrition for my mind and my body. These services granted to me by the English language would never be granted by other majors like philosophy or geography.

So, this is the secret of my growth and prosperity since I acquired English. English gave me access to many individuals' hearts, minds, and consciences. My mastery of the English language sharpened my persuasive skills, which enabled me to open the closed hearts and minds of many individuals who saw the world from a single, narrow perspective. I achieved that mission that was considered impossible in the past with the help of the English language.

Let's not talk too much in this symbolic style and get down to the direct style. However, Aristotle, the great Greek philosopher, once wrote: "to be a master of *metaphor* (a very advanced writing style) is a sign of genius (someone very clever)." I am not trying to be a genius, but my sole purpose is to share with you my outlook and my philosophy in how to overcome life's hardships and difficulties. And one more important philosophy I am trying to share with you is how you can fight with words instead of bullets.

In every story there is a moral, a lesson, and in my *Story with English,* there are many lessons. My story includes my struggle to survive in the English major, and my efforts to be a good and worthy teacher of English. In my desperate fight to win over English and graduate from the English Department, I have narrated with pain and tears how I survived and graduated from the English Department. My success that seemed to me in the beginning something unachievable, became real. And as Edison said: "Successes result from failures." It must be admitted that I was a legendary student.

So, from a legendary student to a legendary teacher. What made me think that I am a legendary teacher is my unshaken belief that: "We learn from cradle to grave." I have never missed any chance to learn something innovative in teaching and learning whenever I came across it. I always valued my peers' observations, opinions, and their friendly criticism of my teaching. I have never failed to give serious consideration to my students' suggestions and opinions about me and the sessions. My door is always open and the classroom is not a holy place.

Besides, the classroom for me is not just a place for learning something or for passing the exam, in fact, it is a social place, an emotional place and a miniature of the outside world. My students rarely rushed out of the classroom at the end of the session. I am sure you understand why. And when I became a storyteller, my classroom became one of my students' most favourite *coffee shops.*

With time, I developed a great passion for teaching, and once you are passionate about what you teach, you will become a legendary teacher. Passion, in my point of view and in the view of many others, is one of the pillars of successful teaching. Besides, once you demonstrate that you are passionate about what you teach, your students become prone to develop passion for that subject as well. Passion is contagious. This is a recipe for success in one of the most challenging professions in the world, teaching.

My difficult journey with the English language in all its phases as a learner, as a teacher, and as an author made me develop my own theories of teaching and learning. Once you have read this book, you will have tapped a treasure trove.

But one thing I want to stress is that mastery of any a language, especially a global language like English, is a great contribution to spreading peace in the world, to spreading understanding among people from different backgrounds and cultures, and to spreading prosperity and opportunities for earning a living among world's citizens. Can you guess the number of people in the world who earn their living because of the English language?

You must have read in previous chapters about my desperate attempts to join higher education to teach English to undergraduates to escape from teaching *devils* at the Technical Secondary School before they *devoured* me. For two years, my job applications contained their death warrant, and that was my *poor and unimpressive* License to teach English. How on earth did I dare to apply for a teaching position in a higher educational institution without an MA or even an appropriate BA? Who would employ you with such a poor unimpressive License to teach English? Who would even care to look at your unimpressive application when applications with PhDs and MAs are falling on HR Heads? Besides, you were one of those English teachers at government schools who were well known for being incompetent and almost ignorant of the English language. That was another death warrant. But despite all those death warrants, I saved myself and obtained a position at a higher education college.

But who was behind me and helped me come back to life? The answer is:

It was my *powerful English language* that defeated the interview panel and made my poor unimpressive teaching license *obsolete*—no longer needed. Just as that Chief Engineer at the American company in Oran some years earlier *employed me at the end of the interview* without any hesitation. He did not bother to look at my BA because he was *impressed by my English* and my performance, and thus my certificate was not needed, in his opinion. "This is how we deal with things in America," he said.

All of a sudden, my *powerful English* transformed me from a poor schoolteacher into a member of staff at a respected college mixing with colleagues from all over the world, some holding PhDs, some holding MAs, and some had graduated from the finest universities in the world. While sitting with this elite on leather seats round mahogany tables in the board rooms, I felt elated and special. But my moment of greatness materialised when these global intellectuals approached me for information and advice. I, that poor English school teacher, have become a source of *invaluable information* to some of the most educated individuals in the world.

Poem

I have written this poem as a dedication to **My First English Teacher** to express my profound love and respect.

A Tribute to My First English Teacher

My First English Teacher was a legend.
He taught in a way no other teachers had envisioned.
His unique teaching strategy, in the history of teaching, no one possessed.
He always entered the classroom with a broad shining smile.
While other teachers entered with a frowning face and a whip.
To smile at devils like us was not their style.

My First English Teacher carried maps, pictures, and posters,
Telling us, "Boys if you learn English well,
you will reach the world's corners."
He made us dream of exotic lands day and night,
And every word he taught us brought into our life
more fun, more joy, more success, and more light.

My First English Teacher opened our hearts and minds,
And filled them with curiosity and questions of all kinds.
He spread the world's map on the wall,
He pointed to countries in south and north
That grabbed the attention of everyone and all.

Before we met our First English Teacher
we used to think,
the world, like our village,
was too small and had no link.

My First English Teacher made English our sail ships
The more verbs, the more nouns, the more adjectives.
He urged, "These will make you faster and get you more winds."
He said, "Learn English to conquer the world,
In this battle, you will fight bravely with every English word.
The more words, the more strength, and a chance to fly like a bird."

My First English Teacher was the wisest of the wise,
He said to us,
"Your English will fill your hearts with sympathy and love,
And you will fly over the world, not a falcon but a peaceful dove.
People everywhere will wave at you and send you flowers and kisses,
They are so pleased to be your friends."

I want to send My First English Teacher
my warm and hearty greeting and
my deep gratitude for his super unmatched teaching.

"My First English Teacher,
I am indebted to you my whole life,
For giving me a vision, a right path, and a dream.
And an English effective weapon that made *'Peace and Love'*
My everyday theme."